AF419977

Contents

Introduction

Popularly known as the First Citizen of the 18th Century, Benjamin Franklin was a famous American writer, inventor, politician, statesman, author, scientist, diplomat and civic activist among many other profiles that he held in his lifetime. As a young boy, Franklin apprenticed with his printer brother. The opportunity gave him the much needed exposure to new ideas and ideals. He grew up to become an inventor and is best known till date for his work in electrical theory. He established the laws by which electricity operates and also conducted crucial inventions including the Lightning rod and Franklin stove. As a diplomat, he was widely admired among the French and was a major figure in the development of Franco-American relations. As a politician, Franklin still stands as America's most effective statesman and ambassador. He was undoubtedly American's most influential Founding Fathers who drafted the Declaration of Independence and the Constitution of the United States.

Given here is a compilation of some of the best known quotes by Benjamin Franklin covering a wide variety of aspectslike life, truth, education, learning, happiness, anger, finance, and so on. Brief yourself and get inspired by his greatness!

BENJAMIN FRANKLIN QUOTES

➢ Whoever would overthrow the liberty of a nation must begin by subduing the freeness of speech.

➢ If everyone is thinking alike, then no one is thinking.

➢ Revolution... War is when the government tells you who the bad guy is. Revolution is when you decide that for yourself.

➢ Hunger never saw bad bread.

➢ He who would trade liberty for some temporary security, deserves neither liberty nor security.

➢ We are all born ignorant, but one must work hard to remain stupid.

➢ It is the first responsibility of every citizen to question authority.

➢ The best thing to give to your enemy is forgiveness; to an opponent, tolerance; to a friend, your heart; to your child, a good example; to a father, deference; to your

mother, conduct that will make her proud of
you; to yourself, respect; to all others, charity.

➢ When you get into a tight place and everything
goes against you, till it seems as though you
could not hold on a minute longer, never give
up then, for that is just the place and time that
the tide will turn. When you're down to
nothing, God is up to something. The faithful
see the invisible, believe the incredible and then
receive the impossible. Where liberty dwells
there is my country.

➢ Make yourself sheep and the wolves will eat
you.

➢ Little minds think and talk about people.
Average minds think and talk about things and
actions. Great minds think and talk about ideas.

➢ Security without liberty is called prison.

➢ Genius is nothing but a greater aptitude for
patience.

➢ Life's Tragedy is that we get old too soon and
wise too late.

➢ Tricks and treachery are the practice of fools,
that don't have brains enough to be honest.

➢ Only a virtuous people are capable of freedom.
As nations become corrupt and vicious, they
have more need of masters.

➢ Instead of cursing the darkness, light a candle.

➢ This [the U.S. Constitution] is likely to be
administered for a course of years and then end
in despotism... when the people shall become
so corrupted as to need despotic government,
being incapable of any other.

➢ Remember not only to say the right thing in the
right place, but far more difficult still, to leave
unsaid the wrong thing at the tempting
moment.

➢ For every minute spent in organizing, an hour is
earned.

➢ The heart of a fool is in his mouth, but the
mouth of a wise man is in his heart.

➢ There are two ways to increase your wealth. Increase your means or decrease your wants. The best is to do both at the same time.

➢ The problem with doing nothing is not knowing when you're finished.

➢ If you would persuade, you must appeal to interest rather than intellect.

➢ Reading makes a full man, meditation a profound man, discourse a clear man.

➢ Believe none of what you hear and half of what you see.

➢ I never knew a man who was good at making excuses who was good at anything else.

➢ Those who beat their swords into plowshares usually end up plowing for those who kept their swords.

➢ Either write something worth reading or do something worth writing.

➢ The only thing that is more expensive than education is ignorance.

➢ Fear God, and your enemies will fear you.

➢ If you do tomorrow what you did today , you will get tomorrow what you got today

➢ Common sense is something that everyone needs, few have, and none think they lack.

➢ How do you become better tomorrow? By improving yourself, the world is made better. Be not afraid of growing too slowly. Be afraid of standing still. Forget your mistakes, but remember what they taught you. So how do you become better tomorrow? By becoming better today.

➢ Change is the only constant in life. Ones ability to adapt to those changes will determine your success in life.

➢ Common sense without education, is better than education without common sense.

➢ The world is run by the people who show up.

➢ In free governments the rulers are the servants, and the people their superiors and sovereigns.

➢ Never ruin an apology with an excuse.

➢ All highly competent people continually search for ways to keep learning, growing, and improving. They do that by asking WHY. After all, the person who knows HOW will always have a job, but the person who knows WHY will always be the boss.

➢ Justice will not be served until those who are unaffected are as outraged as those who are.

➢ The U. S. Constitution doesn't guarantee happiness, only the pursuit of it. You have to catch up with it yourself.

➢ Thirteen virtues necessary for true success: temperance, silence, order, resolution, frugality, industry, sincerity, justice, moderation, cleanliness, tranquility, chastity, and humility.

➢ The ordaining of laws in favor of one part of the nation, to the prejudice and oppression of another, is certainly the most erroneous and mistaken policy. An equal dispensation of protection, rights, privileges, and advantages, is what every part is entitled to, and ought to enjoy.

- ➤ A good example is the best sermon.

- ➤ Freedom is not a gift bestowed upon us by other men, but a right that belongs to us by the laws of God and nature.

- ➤ Take the money in your wallet and invest it in your mind. And in return, your mind will fill up your wallet!

- ➤ The best of all medicines is resting and fasting

- ➤ I am for doing good to the poor, but I differ in opinion about the means. I think the best way of doing good to the poor is not making them easy in poverty, but leading or driving them out of it.

- ➤ Rebellion against tyrants is obedience to God.

- ➤ Doing your best means never stop trying.

- ➤ The best tranquilizer is a clear conscience.

- ➤ Without freedom of thought, there can be no such thing as wisdom; and no such thing as public liberty without freedom of speech; which is the right of every man as far as by it he does not hurt or control the right of another; and this is the only check it ought to suffer and the only bounds it ought to know.... Whoever would overthrow the liberty of a nation must begin by subduing the freedom of speech, a thing terrible to traitors.

➢ To find out a girl's faults, praise her to her girlfriends.

➢ Any fool can criticize, condemn and complain - and most fools do.

➢ If you want to make a friend, let someone do you a favor.

➢ The rapid progress of the sciences makes me sorry, at times, that I was born so soon. Imagine the power that man will have over matter, a few hundred years from now. We may learn how to remove gravity from large masses, and float them over great distances. Agriculture will double its produce with less labor. All diseases will surely be cured... even old age. If only the moral sciences could be improved as well. Perhaps men would cease to be wolves to one another... and human beings could learn to be human.

- ➢ Genius is the ability to hold one's vision steady until it becomes reality

- ➢ Be cheerful -- the problems that worry us most are those that never arrive.

- ➢ Freedom of speech is a principal pillar of a free government; when this support is taken away, the constitution of a free society is dissolved, and tyranny is erected on its ruins. Republics and limited monarchies derive their strength and vigor from a popular examination into the action of the magistrates.

- ➢ I have lived, Sir, a long time and the longer I live, the more convincing proofs I see of this truth -- that God governs in the affairs of men. And if a sparrow cannot fall to the ground without his notice, is it probable that an empire can rise without his aid? We have been assured, Sir, in the sacred writings that "except the Lord build they labor in vain that build it." I firmly believe this; and I also believe that without his concurring aid we shall succeed in this political building no better than the Builders of Babel

- Two passions have powerful influence on the affairs of men: the love of power and the love of money.

- If better is possible, good is not enough

- Being ignorant is not so much a shame, as being unwilling to learn.

- Here is my Creed. I believe in one God, creator of the Universe. That he governs it by his Providence. That he ought to be worshiped. That the most acceptable service we render him is doing good to his other children. That the soul of Man is immortal, and will be treated with justice in another life respecting its conduct in this.

- Beer is proof that God wants us to be happy

- The man who does things makes mistakes, but he doesn't make the biggest mistake of all- doing nothing.

- They that can give up essential liberty to purchase a little temporary safety, deserve neither liberty nor safety.

> Well done is better than well said.

> Success is the residue of planning.

> A nation of well-informed men who have been taught to know and prize the rights which God has given them cannot be enslaved. It is in the region of ignorance that tyranny begins."

> Lost time is never found again.

> Beware of little expenses. A small leak will sink a great ship.

> Man will ultimately be governed by God or by tyrants.

> Motivation is when your dreams put on work clothes

> Those who would give up essential Liberty, to purchase a little temporary Safety, deserve neither Liberty nor Safety.

> How few there are who have courage enough to own their faults, or resolution enough to mend them.

- Women are books, and men the readers be.

- Money has never made man happy, nor will it, there is nothing in its nature to produce happiness. The more of it one has the more one wants.

- Most men die from the neck up at age twenty-five because they stop dreaming.

- To lengthen thy life, lessen thy meals.

- There are many roads to success, but only one sure road to failure; and that is to try to please everyone else.

- By improving yourself, the world is made better. Be not afraid of growing too slowly. Be afraid only of standing still.

- Who is wise? He that learns from everyone. Who is powerful? He that governs his passions. Who is rich? He that is content. Who is that? Nobody.

- Never confuse motion with action.

- Your argument is sound, nothing but sound.

➢ Out of adversity comes opportunity.

➢ When you are good to others, you are best to yourself.

➢ Your net worth to the world is usually determined by what remains after your bad habits are subtracted from your good ones.

➢ Half the truth is often a great lie.

➢ When you're finished changing, you're finished.

➢ To succeed, jump as quickly at opportunities as you do at conclusions.

➢ The man that walks wit crowd, will get no farther than the crowd. The man that walks alone, will reach places unknown.

➢ There seem to be but three ways for a nation to acquire wealth. The first is by war, as the Romans did, in plundering their conquered neighbors. This is robbery. The second by commerce, which is generally cheating. The third by agriculture, the only honest way, wherein man receives a real increase of the

seed thrown into the ground, in a kind of
continual miracle, wrought by the hand of God
in his favor, as a reward for his innocent life and
his virtuous industry.

➢ Whatever is begun in anger ends in shame.

➢ You must always be prepared. Make sure to
look at things from all angles. If you are not
prepared you will fail.

➢ A people who chose security over liberty will
receive neither nor deserve either.

➢ The way to secure peace is to be prepared for
war. They that are on their guard, and appear
ready to receive their adversaries, are in much
less danger of being attacked, than the supine,
secure, and negligent.

➢ Most men die at 25, we just don't bury them
until they are 70.

➢ In my youth, I traveled much, and I observed in
different countries, that the more public
provisions were made for the poor, the less
they provided for themselves, and of course
became poorer. And, on the contrary, the less

was done for them, the more they did for themselves, and became richer.

> The height of foolishness is to discard an opportunity without full investigation

> Repeal that welfare law, and you will soon see a change in their manners. ... Six days shalt thou labor, though one of the old commandments long treated as out of date, will again be looked upon as a respectable precept; industry will increase, and with it plenty among the lower people; their circumstances will mend, and more will be done for their happiness by inuring them to provide for themselves, than could be done by dividing all your estates among them.

> Without Freedom of thought there can be no such thing as wisdom;and no such thing as public liberty, without freedom of speech.

> If you want something done, ask a busy person.

> Wish not so much to live long as to live well.

> Happiness depends more on the inward disposition of mind than on outward circumstances.

- ➢ The best doctor gives the least medicines.

- ➢ He that would live in peace and at ease, must not speak all he knows nor judge all he sees.

- ➢ I am a mortal enemy to arbitrary government and unlimited power. I am naturally very jealous for the rights and liberties of my country, and the least encroachment of those invaluable privileges is apt to make my blood boil.

- ➢ When the well is dry, we know the worth of water.

- ➢ He that cannot obey, cannot command.

- ➢ Do not anticipate trouble, or worry about what may never happen. Keep in the sunlight.

- ➢ An investment in knowledge pays the best interest. When it comes to investing, nothing will pay off more than educating yourself. Do the necessary research, study and analysis before making any investment decisions.

- ➢ He that is good for making excuses is seldom good for anything else.

➢ You may delay, but time will not.

➢ If you watch your pennies, the pounds will take care of themselves.

➢ History affords us many instances of the ruin of states, by the prosecution of measures ill suited to the temper and genius of their people. The ordaining of laws in favor of one part of the nation, to the prejudice and oppression of another, is certainly the most erroneous and mistaken policy. ... These measures never fail to create great and violent jealousies and animosities between the people favored and the people oppressed; whence a total separation of affections, interests, political obligations, and all manner of connections, by which the whole state is weakened.

➢ The way to be safe is never to be secure.

➢ Beware of the young doctor and the old barber.

➢ He that is of the opinion money will do everything may well be suspected of doing everything for money.

- ➢ Those who laugh often never grow old.

- ➢ The noblest question in the world is: 'What good may I do in it?'

- ➢ How many observe Christ's birthday! How few, His precepts!

- ➢ Be studious in your profession, and you will be learned. Be industrious and frugal, and you will be rich. Be sober and temperate, and you will be healthy. Be in general virtuous, and you will be happy.

- ➢ A good conscience is a continual Christmas.

- ➢ That which hurts, also instructs.

- ➢ Sell not virtue to purchase wealth, nor liberty to purchase power.

- ➢ If you fail to plan, you are planning to fail!

- ➢ The learned fool writes his nonsense in better language than the unlearned, but it is still nonsense.

- ➢ whatever you become be good at it

- Sin is not hurtful because it is forbidden, but it is forbidden because it is hurtful.

- The way to see by Faith is to shut the Eye of Reason.

- Among the numerous luxuries of the table...coffee may be considered as one of the most valuable. It excites cheerfulness without intoxication; and the pleasing flow of spirits which it occasions...is never followed by sadness, languor or debility.

- Fart for freedom, fart for liberty—and fart proudly.

- Who is wise? He that learns from everyone.

- We constantly change the world, even by our inaction. Therefore, let us change it responsibly.

- A lie stands on one leg, truth on two.

- A long life may not be good enough, but a good life is long enough.

- ➢ A false friend and a shadow attend only while the sun shines.

- ➢ Educate your children to self-control, to the habit of holding passion and prejudice and evil tendencies subject to an upright and reasoning will, and you have done much to abolish misery from their future and crimes from society.

- ➢ Guests, like fish, begin to smell after three days.

- ➢ Love your Enemies, for they tell you your Faults.

- ➢ Who is strong? He that can conquer his bad habits.

- ➢ People are best convinced by things they themselves discover.

- ➢ The great secret of succeeding in conversation is to admire little, to hear much; always to distrust our own reason, and sometimes that of our friends; never to pretend to wit, but to make that of others appear as much as possibly we can; to hearken to what is said and to answer to the purpose.

- ➢ He that displays too often his wife and his wallet is in danger of having both of them borrowed.

- ➢ Rather go to bed with out dinner than to rise in debt.

- ➢ God heals, and the doctor takes the fees.

- ➢ The strictest law sometimes becomes the severest injustice.

- ➢ Don't judge men's wealth or godliness by their Sunday appearance.

- ➢ Early to bed and early to rise makes a man healthy, wealthy and wise.

- ➢ Speak ill of no man, but speak all the good you know of everybody.

- ➢ There are three things extremely hard: steel, a diamond, and to know one's self.

- ➢ Every pot must sit on its own bottom.

- ➢ I believe long habits of virtue have a sensible effect on the countenance.

➢ Lose no time; be always employed in something useful.

➢ Eat to live, not live to eat.

➢ Time is money'... Waste it now. Pay for it later!

➢ There are three sorts of people in the world: Those who are immovable, people who don't get it, or don't want to do anything about it; there are people who are movable, people who see the need for change and are prepared to listen to it; and there are people who move, people who make things happen.

➢ The doorstep to the temple of wisdom is a knowledge of our own ignorance.

➢ People willing to trade their freedom for temporary security deserve neither and will lose both.

➢ Plough deep while sluggards sleep.

➢ You will find the key to success under the alarm clock.

➢ The doors of wisdom are never shut.

➢ I wake up every morning at nine and grab for the morning paper. Then I look at the obituary page. If my name is not on it, I get up.

➢ you can do anything you set your mind to

➢ Outside Independence Hall when the Constitutional Convention of 1787 ended, Mrs. Powel of Philadelphia asked Benjamin Franklin, "Well, Doctor, what have we got, a republic or a monarchy?" With no hesitation whatsoever, Franklin responded, "A republic, if you can keep it."

➢ It is hard for an empty bag to stand upright.

➢ Great beauty, great strength, and great riches are really and truly of no great use; a right heart exceeds all

➢ Keep conscience clear, then never fear.

➢ Never leave that till tomorrow which you can do today.

➢ Diligence is the mother of good luck.

➤ There is much difference between imitating a good man and counterfeiting him.

➤ In these sentiments, sir, I agree to this Constitution, with all its faults, if they are such; because I think a General Government necessary for us, and there is no form of government, but what may be a blessing to the people if well administered; and believe further, that this is likely to be well administered for a course of years, and can only end in despotism, as other forms have done before it, when the people shall become so corrupted as to need despotic government, being incapable of any other.

➤ I didn't fail the test, I just found 100 ways to do it wrong.

➤ God grant, that not only the Love of Liberty, but a thorough Knowledge of the Rights of Man, may pervade all the Nations of the Earth, so that a Philosopher may set his Foot anywhere on its Surface, and say, 'This is my Country.'

➤ A Brother may not be a Friend, but a Friend will always be a Brother.

➢ Freedom of speech is the great bulwark of liberty; they prosper and die together: And it is the terror of traitors and oppressors, and a barrier against them. It produces excellent writers, and encourages men of fine genius.

➢ Clean your finger before you point at my spots.

➢ If by the liberty of the press were understood merely the liberty of discussing the propriety of public measures and political opinions, let us have as much of it as you please: But if it means the liberty of affronting, calumniating and defaming one another, I, for my part, own myself willing to part with my share of it, whenever our legislators shall please so to alter the law and shall chearfully consent to exchange my liberty of abusing others for the privilege of not being abused myself.

➢ Take time for all things: great haste makes great waste.

➢ An education is the investment with the greatest returns.

- ➢ You can't tell anyone anything. You have to teach people for them to remember. Let the person experience what you are teaching and they will learn.

- ➢ Scarcely was I arrived at fifteen years of age, when, after having doubted in turn of different tenets, according as I found them combated in the different books that I read, I began to doubt of Revelation itself.

- ➢ Everybody's human-everybody makes mistakes. If you laugh it off and keep going and try to give it your best the next time around, people respect that.

- ➢ One day is worth a thousand tomorrows.

- ➢ The way to wealth depends on just two words, industry and frugality.

- ➢ To err is human, to repent divine; to persist devilish.

- ➢ Be at war with your vices, at peace with your neighbors, and let every new year find you a better man.

> Waste neither time nor money, but make the best use of both.

> A learned blockhead is a greater blockhead than an ignorant one.

> Many complain of their memory, few of their judgment.

> The discontented man finds no easy chair.

> Eat what you like, but dress for other people.

> A wise man will desire no more than what he may get justly, use soberly, distribute cheerfully, and leave contently.

> God helps them that help themselves.

> If you want a thing done - go. If not - send.

> Virtue alone is sufficient to make a man great, glorious, and happy.

> Those who desire to give up freedom in order to gain security will not have either one.

- ➢ There is scarce a king in a hundred who would not, if he could, follow the example of Pharoah - get first all the people's money, then all their lands, and then make them and their children servants forever.

- ➢ The tongue offends and the ears get the cuffing

- ➢ Human happiness comes not from infrequent pieces of good fortune, but from the small improvements to daily life.

- ➢ We should make the poor uncomfortable and kick them out of poverty.

- ➢ Money makes money. And the money that makes money makes more money.

- ➢ Content makes poor men rich; discontent makes rich men poor.

- ➢ It is easier to prevent bad habits than to break them.

- ➢ He's the best physician that knows the worthlessness of most medicines.

- ➢ The cat in gloves catches no mice.

> An ounce of prevention is worth a pound of cure.

> Silence - Speak not but what may benefit others or yourself; avoid trifling conversation.

> Speak little, do much.

> He that composes himself is wiser than he that composes a book.

> Hide not your talents. They for use were made. What's a sundial in the shade?

> A good spouse and health is a person's best wealth.

> Many a man thinks he is buying pleasure, when he is really selling himself to it.

> [T]he more public provisions were made for the poor, the less they provided for themselves, and of course became poorer . . . [taking] away from before their eyes the greatest of all inducements to industry, frugality, and sobriety, by giving them a dependence of somewhat else

than a careful accumulation during youth and health for support in age and sickness.

➢ A man must have a good deal of vanity who believes, and a good deal of boldness who affirms, that all the doctrines he holds are true, and all he rejects are false.

➢ He's a fool who cannot conceal his wisdom.

➢ Great hopes make everything great possible

➢ Let each new year find you a better person.

➢ To cease to think creatively is to cease to live

➢ No gains without pains.

➢ Take a coin from your purse and invest it in your mind. It will come pouring out of your mind and overflow your purse.

➢ In other men we faults can spy,/ And blame the mote that dims their eye;/ Each little speck and blemish find;/ To our own stronger errors blind.

- ➢ I fear the man who drinks water and so remembers this morning what the rest of us said last night

- ➢ Little leaks sink the ship.

- ➢ Let the child's first lesson be obedience, and the second will be what thou wilt.

- ➢ It is very hard to dislike someone you have helped

- ➢ Words may show a man's wit but actions his meaning.

- ➢ He that best understands the world, least likes it

- ➢ Trouble knocked at the door, but, hearing laughter, hurried away

- ➢ Be slow in choosing a friend, slower in changing.

- ➢ Poverty wants some things, Luxury many things, Avarice all things

- ➢ Be civil to all; serviceable to many; familiar with few; friend to one; enemy to none.

> Industry pays debts, while despair increases them.

> I have found Christian dogma unintelligible. Early in life, I absenteed myself from Christian assemblies.

> It is better to let 100 criminals go free than to imprison 1 innocent man.

> That there is one God, who made all things. That he governs the world by his providence. That he might be worshipped by adoration, prayer, and thanksgiving. But that the most acceptable service of God is doing good to Man. That the Soul is immortal. And that God will certainly reward virtue and punish vice, either here or hereafter.

> What can laws do without morals?

> I believe there is one Supreme most perfect being. [...] I believe He is pleased and delights in the happiness of those He has created; and since without virtue man can have no happiness in this world, I firmly believe He delights to see me virtuous.

➢ Without continual growth and progress, such words as improvement, achievement, and success have no meaning.

➢ A slip of the foot you may soon recover, but a slip of the tongue you may never get over.

➢ My refusing to eat meat occasioned inconveniency, and I have been frequently chided for my singularity. But my light repast allows for greater progress, for greater clearness of head and quicker comprehension.

➢ At twenty years of age the will reigns; at thirty, the wit; and at forty, the judgment.

➢ Do not fear mistakes. You will know failure. Continue to reach out.

➢ Keep your eyes wide open before marriage, half shut afterwards.

➢ There are three faithful friends - an old wife, an old dog, and ready money.

➢ In 1736 I lost one of my sons, a fine boy of four years old, by the small-pox, taken in the common way. I long regretted bitterly, and still regret that I had not given it to him by inoculation. This I mention for the sake of parents who omit that operation, on the supposition that they should never forgive themselves if a child died under it; my example showing that the regret may be the same either way, and that, therefore, the safer should be chosen.

> Write your injuries in dust, your benefits in marble.

> Those things that hurt, instruct.

> Joy doesn't exist in the world, it exists in us.

> Wise men learn by others' harms, fools scarcely by their own.

> I would advise you to read with a pen in your hand and enter in a little book short hints of what you feel that is common or that may be useful; for this will be the best method of imprinting such portcullis in your memory.

> We are all born without knowledge, but curious. With curiosity we should be able to learn as

much as possible. With curiosity, it has to take a lot of work to remain ignorant.

➤ The Constitution only guarantees the American people the right to pursue happiness. You have to catch it yourself.

➤ A Bible and a newspaper in every house, a good school in every district; all studied and appreciated as they merit; are the principal support of virtue, morality, and civil liberty.

➤ If a man could have half of his wishes, he would double his troubles.

➤ Observe all men, thyself most.

➤ All mankind is divided into three classes: those that are immovable, those that are movable, and those that move.

➤ Leisure is the time for doing something useful.

➤ When circumstances don't fit our ideas they become our difficulties

➤ Time is an herb that cures all Diseases.

- If you wish information and improvement from the knowledge of others, and yet at the same time express yourself as firmly fix'd in your present opinions, modest, sensible men, who do not love disputation, will probably leave you undisturbed in the possession of your error.

- Wars are not paid for in wartime. The bill comes later.

- If you would know the value of money, go and try to borrow some.

- In the dark, all cats are grey.

- Industry need not wish, and he that lives upon hopes will die fasting. There are no gains without pains. He that hath a trade hath an estate, and he that hath a calling hath an office of profit and honor; but then the trade must be worked at and the calling followed, or neither the estate nor the office will enable us to pay our taxes. If we are industrious, we shall never starve; for at the workingman's house hunger looks in, but dares not enter. Nor will the bailiff or the constable enter, for industry pays debts, while idleness and neglect increase them.

➢ Beware of meat twice boiled, and an old foe reconciled.

➢ The securest place is a prison cell, but there is no liberty

➢ Industry, perseverance, and frugality make fortune yield.

➢ Wise men don't need advice. Fools won't take it.

➢ As to Jesus of Nazareth, my opinion of whom you particularly desire, I think the system of Morals and his Religion, as he left them to us, the best the World ever saw or is likely to see; but I apprehend it has received various corrupting Changes; and I have, with most of the present Dissenters in England, some doubts as to his divinity.

➢ But the most dangerous Hypocrite in a Common-Wealth, is one who leaves the Gospel for the sake of the Law: A Man compounded of Law and Gospel, is able to cheat a whole Country with his Religion, and then destroy them under Colour of Law: And here the Clergy are in great Danger of being deceiv'd, and the

People of being deceiv'd by the Clergy, until the Monster arrives to such Power and Wealth, that he is out of the reach of both, and can oppress the People without their own blind Assistance.

➢ The best investment is in the tools of one's own trade.

➢ In New England they once thought blackbirds useless, and mischievous to the corn. They made efforts to destroy them. The consequence was, the blackbirds were diminished; but a kind of worm, which devoured their grass, and which the blackbirds used to feed on, increased prodigiously; then, finding their loss in grass much greater than their saving in corn, they wished again for their blackbirds.

➢ An investment in knowledge pays the best interest.

➢ To be humble to superiors is a duty, to equals courtesy, to inferiors nobleness.

➢ The rotten apple spoils his companion.

➢ Moderation in all things - including moderation.

- Promises may get thee friends, but non-performance will turn them into enemies.

- Whoever shall introduce into public affairs the principles of primitive Christianity will change the face of the world.

- Why ruin a young girl's life when you can make an older women SO very happy !

- Three may keep a secret, if two of them are dead.

- He was so learned that he could name a horse in nine languages; so ignorant that he bought a cow to ride on.

- For having lived long, I have experienced many instances of being obliged, by better information or fuller consideration, to change opinions, even on important subjects, which I once thought right but found to be otherwise.

- Thank God! we are in the full enjoyment of all these privileges. But can we be taught to prize them too much? or how can we prize them equal to their value, if we do not know their intrinsic worth, and that they are not a gift

bestowed upon us by other men, but a right
that belongs to us by the laws of God and
nature?

➤ It is a bad temper of mind that takes delight in
opposition.

➤ Disdain the chain, preserve your freedom; and
maintain your independency: be industrious
and free; be frugal and free.

➤ There is no little enemy

➤ He that is rich need not live sparingly, and he
that can live sparingly need not be rich.

➤ In the beginning of the contest with Britain,
when we were sensible of danger, we had daily
prayers in this room for Divine protection," he
stated. "Our prayers, Sir, were heard, and they
were graciously answered. ... Do we imagine we
no longer need His assistance?

➤ After all, wedlock is the natural state of man. A
bachelor is not a complete human being. He is
like the odd half of a pair of scissors, which has
not yet found its fellow, and therefore is not
even half so useful as they might be together.

> You made delay, but time will not, and lost time is never found again.

> There never was a good war, or a bad peace.

> They who can give up essential liberty to obtain a little temporary safety deserve neither liberty nor safety.

> There never was a truly great man that was not at the same time truly virtuous.

> By playing at Chess then, we may learn: First: Foresight... Second: Circumspection... Third: Caution...And lastly, we learn by Chess the habit of not being discouraged by present bad appearances in the state of our affairs, the habit of hoping for a favorable chance, and that of persevering in the secrets of resources

> Who is rich? He that rejoices in his portion.

> Pride that dines on vanity, sups on contempt.

> Lighthouses are more helpful than churches.

- ➢ The only time a question should be asked is when all other possibilities of finding the answer for yourself have been eliminated.

- ➢ Creditors have better memories than debtors.

- ➢ The problem with common sense is, it isn't.

- ➢ Nothing is more fatal to health than an over care of it.

- ➢ Our whole life is but a greater and longer childhood.

- ➢ He that speaks much, is much mistaken.

- ➢ In success be moderate. Humility makes great men twice honourable.

- ➢ Don't put off until tomorrow what you can do today.

- ➢ If Men are so wicked as we now see them with Religion what would they be if without it?

- ➢ Reckless youth makes rueful age.

➢ One of the greatest tragedies of life is the murder of a beautiful theory by a gang of brutal facts.

➢ When men differ in opinion, both sides ought equally to have the advantage of being heard by the public; when Truth and Error have fair play, the former is always an overmatch for the latter.

➢ Masonic labor is purely a labor of love. He who seeks to draw Masonic wages in gold and silver will be disappointed. The wages of a Mason are in the dealings with one another; sympathy begets sympathy, kindness begets kindness, helpfulness begets helpfulness, and these are the wages of a Mason.

➢ He that won't be counseled can't be helped.

➢ A penny saved is a penny earned.

➢ The second vice is lying, the first is running in debt.

➢ Marriage is the most natural state of man, and therefore the state in which one is most likely to find solid happiness.

- ➢ Silence is not always a sign of wisdom, but babbling is ever a mark of folly.

- ➢ The absent are never without fault. Nor the present without excuse.

- ➢ Sloth, like rust, consumes faster than labor wears, while the used key is always bright.

- ➢ It is the religion of ignorance that tyranny begins.

- ➢ If you have time don't wait for time.

- ➢ Remember, that six pounds a year is but a groat a day.

- ➢ A man wrapped up in himself makes a very small bundle.

- ➢ None but the well-bred man knows how to confess a fault, or acknowledge himself in an error.

- ➢ By playing at Chess then, we may learn... First: Foresight. Second: Circumspection. Third: Caution.

> Many foxes grow gray but few grow good.

> When you speak to a man, look on his eyes; when he speaks to you, look on his mouth.

> There will be sleeping enough in the grave.

> I have sometimes almost wished it had been my destiny to be born two or three centuries hence.

> When you incline to have new clothes, look first well over the old ones, and see if you cannot shift with them another year, either by scouring, mending, or even patching if necessary. Remember, a patch on your coat, and money in your pocket, is better and more creditable, than a writ on your back, and no money to take it off.

> He that goes a borrowing goes a sorrowing.

> If you would be wealthy, think of saving as well as getting.

> Remember that credit is money.

- It is better to take many injuries than to give one.

- If you know how to spend less than you get, you have the philosopher's stone.

- Pen, wax and parchment govern the world.

- A little neglect may breed great mischief. ... For want of a nail, the shoe was lost; for want of a shoe, the horse was lost; for want of a horse, the battle was lost; for want of the battle, the war was lost.

- Happiness consists more in small conveniences or pleasures that occur every day, than in great pieces of good fortune that happen but seldom to a man in the course of his life.

- Nothing preaches better than the act.

- I therefore beg leave to move that henceforth prayers imploring the assistance of Heaven, and its blessing on our deliberations, be held in this Assembly every morning.

- He is not well bred, that cannot bear ill breeding in others

> Eat few suppers, and you'll need few medicines.

> Women and wine, game and deceit, make the wealth small, and the want great

> If you would keep your secret from an enemy, tell it not to a friend.

> Where sense is wanting, everything is wanting.

> But our great security lies, I think, in our growing strength.

> If you do not exclude them, in less than 200 years our descendants will be working in the fields to furnish them substance, while they will be in the counting houses rubbing their hands. I warn you, gentlemen, if you do not exclude Jews for all time, your children will curse you in your graves.

> Practice makes perfect.

> Pardoning the Bad, is injuring the Good.

> If I could see one live show before I died, I'd see Lucy Angel

➢ He that can have patience can have what he will.

➢ Necessity never made a good bargain.

➢ Behold the rain which descends from heaven upon our vineyards; there it enters the roots of the vines, to be changed into wine; a constant proof that God loves us, and loves to see us happy.

➢ If you teach a poor young man to shave himself, and keep his razor in order, you may contribute more to the happiness of his life than in giving him a thousand guineas.

➢ One good husband is worth two good wives, for the scarcer things are, the more they are valued.

➢ No European who has tasted savage life can afterwards bear to live in our societies.

➢ Don't go to the doctor with every distemper, nor to the lawyer with every quarrel, nor to the pot for every thirst.

➢ Where there is hunger, law is not regarded; and where law is not regarded, there will be hunger.

➢ A quarrelsome man has no good neighbours.

➢ Presumption first blinds a man, then sets him a running.

➢ A full Belly brings forth every Evil.

➢ The world is full of fools and faint hearts; and yet everyone has courage enough to bear the misfortunes, and wisdom enough to manage the affairs, of his neighbor.

➢ Let every fart count as a peal of thunder for liberty. Let every fart remind the nation of how much it has let pass out of its control. It is a small gesture, but one that can be very effective - especially in a large crowd. So fart, and if you must, fart often. But always fart without apology. Fart for freedom, fart for liberty - and fart proudly.

➢ Fatigue is the best pillow.

➢ Pride is said to be the last vice the good man gets clear of.

➢ That is simple. In the Colonies we issue our own money. It is called Colonial Scrip. We issue it in proper proportion to the demands of trade and industry to make the products pass easily from the producers to the consumers. In this manner creating for ourselves our own paper money, we control its purchasing power, and we have no interest to pay.

➢ Eat not to dullness, drink not to elevation.

➢ If you'd be wealthy, think of saving, more than of getting: The Indies have not made Spain rich, because her Outgoes equal her Incomes.

➢ Idle hands are the devil's playthings.

➢ I am lord of myself, accountable to none.

➢ The early morning has gold in its mouth.

➢ A bargain is something you have to find a use for once you have bought it.

➢ Little boats should keep near shore

➢ If you would have a faithful servant, and one that you like, serve yourself.

➢ We are more heavily taxed by our idleness, pride and folly than we are taxed by government.

➢ In America, they do not inquire of a stranger, "What is he?" but, "What can he do?"

➢ You will observe with concern how long a useful truth may be known, and exist, before it is generally received and practiced on.

➢ A house is not a home unless it contains food and fire for the mind as well as the body.

➢ Families ought to be noisy.

➢ I think also, that general virtue is more probably to be expected and obtained from the education of youth, than from exhortations of adult persons; bad habits and vices of the mind being, like diseases of the body, more easily prevented than cured. I think moreover, that talents for the education of youth are the gift of God; and that he on whom they are bestowed, whenever a way is opened for use of them, is as strongly called as if he heard a voice from heaven.

> Take time for all things.

> Here is my Creed. I believe in one God, the Creator of the Universe. That He governs it by His Providence. That He ought to be worshipped.

> An old man in a house is a good sign.

> Be ashamed to catch yourself idle.

> So much for industry, my friends, and attention to one's own business; but to these we must add frugality if we would make our industry more certainly successful. A man may, if he knows not how to save as he gets, keep his nose all his life to the grindstone, and die not worth a grout at last.

> If you teach a poor young man to shave himself, and keep his razor in order, you may contribute more to the happiness of his life than in giving him a thousand guineas. This sum may be soon spent, the regret only remaining of having foolishly consumed it; but in the other case, he

escapes the frequent vexation of waiting for barbers, and of their sometimes dirty fingers, offensive breaths, and dull razors.

➤ Think of these things, whence you came, where you are going, and to whom you must account.

➤ Arguing is a game that two can play at. But it is a strange game in that neither opponent ever wins.

➤ If you have no Honey in your Pot, have some in your Mouth.

➤ If you have something to do tomorrow, do it today.

➤ He that pursues two hares at once, does not catch one and lets the other go.

➤ Those who in quarrels interpose, must often wipe a bloody nose.

➤ Your best investment is to pour your purse into your head, and no one can take it away from you.

➢ I have thought that wild flowers might be the alphabet of angels, — whereby they write on hills and fields mysterious truths, which it is not given our fallen nature to understand.

➢ The best is the cheapest.

➢ He that has done you a kindness will be more ready to do you another, than he whom you yourself have obliged.

➢ All would live long, but none would be old.

➢ Don't you know, that all wives are in the right? It may be you don't, for you are yet a young husband.

➢ In this world nothing can be said to be certain, except death and taxes.

➢ An honest Man will receive neither Money nor Praise that is not his due.

➢ Do good to your friends to keep them, to your enemies to win them.

➢ If you would be loved, love, and be loveable.

➢ Are you angry that others disappoint you? Remember you cannot depend upon yourself.

➢ Flesh eating is unprovoked murder.

➢ Necessity knows no law; I know some attorneys of the same.

➢ Nothing but Money, Is sweeter than Honey.

➢ Look before, or you'll find yourself behind.

➢ Glass, China, and Reputation, are easily cracked, and never well mended.

➢ Laws without morals are in vain.

➢ When you are done changing, you're done.

➢ If you would not be laughed at, be the first to laugh at yourself.

➢ Energy and persistence conquer all things.

➢ A man in a passion, rides a mad horse.

➢ You can not pluck roses without fear of thorns, Nor enjoy a fair wife without danger of horns.

➢ History will also afford frequent opportunities of showing the necessity of a public religion, from its usefulness to the public; the advantage of a religious character among private persons; the mischiefs of superstition, and the excellency of the Christian religion above all others, ancient or modern.

➢ Nature performs the cure, the physician takes the fee.

➢ Reading was the only amusement I allowed myself

➢ I have lived, Sir, a long time, and the longer I live, the more convincing proofs I see of this truth — that God governs in the affairs of men.

➢ Don't throw stones at your neighbors, if your own windows are glass.

➢ When you are in debt, then you are a slave.

➢ Praise little, dispraise less.

➢ I have always thought that one man of tolerable abilities may work great changes, and accomplish great affairs among mankind, if he first forms a good plan, and, cutting off all amusements or other employments that would divert his attention, make the execution of that same plan his sole study and business.

> Hunger is the best pickle.

> Search others for their virtues, thyself for thy vices.

> Anger is never without a reason, but seldom with a good one.

> Sloth makes all things difficult, but industry all easy; and he that riseth late must trot all day, and shall scarce overtake his business at night; while laziness travels so slowly, that poverty soon overtakes him.

> Alas, I know if I ever became truly humble, I would be proud of it.

> Lying rides upon debt's back.

> Drive your business. Let not your business drive you.

- ➤ Sloth and Silence are a Fool's Virtues

- ➤ The borrower is a slave to the lender and the debtor to the creditor.

- ➤ The proof of gold is fire.

- ➤ Don't misinform your Doctor nor your Lawyer.

- ➤ Enjoy the present hour, be mindful of the past; And neither fear nor wish the Approaches of the last. Learn of the skillful: He that teaches himself, hath a fool for his master.

- ➤ An old young man, will be a young old man.

- ➤ The poor have little; beggars, none; the rich, too much; enough, not one.

- ➤ Fish and visitors stink in three days.

- ➤ Write to Please Yourself. When You write to Please Others You end up Pleasing No one.

- ➤ Without justice, courage is weak.

- ➤ If you can't pay for a thing, don't buy it. If you can't get paid for it, don't sell it. Do this, and you will have calm and drowsy nights, with all of the good business you have now and none of the bad. If you have time, don't wait for time.

➢ Dost thou love life? Then do not squander time, for that is the stuff life is made of.

➢ He that lives well, is learned enough.

➢ The person who deserves most pity is a lonesome one on a rainy day who doesn't know how to read.

➢ Be studious in your profession, and you will be learned. Be industrious and frugal, and you will be rich. Be sober and temperate, and you will be healthy. Be in general virtuous, and you will be happy. At least you will, by such conduct, stand the be.

➢ The way to wealth is as plain as the way to market. It depends chiefly on two words, industry and frugality: that is, waste neither time nor money, but make the best use of both. Without industry and frugality nothing will do, and with them everything.

➢ Only a virtuous people are capable of freedom.

- It is the working man who is the happy man. It is the idle man who is the miserable man.

- Laws too gentle are seldom obeyed; too severe, seldom executed.

- Experience is the best teacher, but a fool will learn from no other.

- I have so much faith in the general government of the world by Providence that I can hardly conceive a transaction of such momentous importance [as the framing of the Constitution] ... should be suffered to pass without being in some degree influenced, guided, and governed by that omnipotent, omnipresent, and beneficent Ruler in whom all inferior spirits live and move and have their being.

- The busy man has few idle visitors; to the boiling pot the flies come not.

- Quacks are the greatest liars in the world except their patients.

- You may give give a man office, but you cannot give him discretion

➢ He that is conscious of a stink in his breeches is [suspicious] of every wrinkle in another's nose.

➢ Take one thing with another, and the world is a pretty good sort of a world, and it is our duty to make the best of it, and be thankful.

➢ But the eyes of other people are the eyes that ruin us. If all but myself were blind, I should want neither fine clothes, fine houses nor fine furniture.

➢ The one who fails to prepare is preparing to fail.

➢ If you wou'd have Guests merry with your cheer, Be so your self, or so at least appear.

➢ There's small Revenge in Words, but Words may be greatly revenged

➢ What I am to be, I am now becoming.

➢ It takes many good deeds to build a good reputation, and only one bad one to lose it.

➢ After three days men grow weary, of a wench, a guest, and weather rainy.

➢ Rarely use Venery but for Health or Offspring; Never to Dulness, Weakness, or the Injury of your own or another's Peace or Reputation.

➢ In reality, there is, perhaps, no one of our natural passions so hard to subdue as pride. Disguise it, struggle with it, beat it down, stifle it, mortify it as much as one pleases, it is still alive, and will every now and then peep out and show itself; you will see it, perhaps, often in this history; for, even if I could conceive that I had completely overcome it, I should probably be proud of my humility.

➢ Do not do that which you would not have known.

➢ It is the duty of mankind on all suitable occasions to acknowledge their dependence on the Divine Being... Almighty God would mercifully interpose and still the rage of war among the nations... He would take this province under His protection, confound the designs and defeat the attempts of its enemies, and unite our hearts and strengthen our hands in every undertaking that may be for the public

good, and for our defense and security in this
time of danger.

➢ Temperance puts wood on the fire, meal in the
barrel, flour in the tub, money in the purse,
credit in the country, contentment in the house,
clothes on the back, and vigor in the body.

➢ The honest Man takes Pains, and then enjoys
Pleasures; the knave takes Pleasure, and then
suffers Pains.

➢ Let the experiment be made.

➢ Fools need advice most, but wise men only are
the better for it.

➢ The use of money is all the advantage there is in
having money.

➢ Each year one vicious habit discarded, in time
might make the worst of us good.

➢ An investment in education always pays the
highest returns.

➢ Death takes no bribes.

> Read much, but not too many books.

> Make use of your friends by being of use to them.

> Admiration is the daughter of ignorance.

> After getting the first hundred pounds, it is more easy to get the second.

> The same man cannot be both Friend and Flatterer.

> God helps those who help themselves.

> Perhaps the history of the errors of mankind, all things considered, is more valuable and interesting than that of their discoveries. Truth is uniform and narrow; it constantly exists, and does not seem to require so much an active energy, as a passive aptitude of the soul in order to encounter it. But error is endlessly diversified; it has no reality, but is the pure and simple creation of the mind that invents it. In this field the soul has room enough to expand herself, to display all her boundless faculties, and all her beautiful and interesting extravagancies and absurdities.

➢ Be sober and temperate, and you will be healthy.

➢ The devil wipes his breech with poor folks' pride.

➢ Spare when young, and spend when old.

➢ You cannot always run from a weakness. You must sometime fight it out or perish.

➢ I firmly believe this ... that without His concurring aid we shall succeed in this political building no better, than the builders of Babel: We shall be divided by our little partial local interests; our projects will be confounded, and we ourselves shall become a reproach and bye word down to future ages. And what is worse, mankind may hereafter from this unfortunate instance, despair of establishing governments by human wisdom and leave it to chance, war and conquest.

➢ If you wou'd be reveng'd of your enemy, govern your self

➤ [E]very Man who comes among us, and takes up a piece of Land, becomes a Citizen, and by our Constitution has a Voice in Elections, and a share in the Government of the Country.

➤ On being asked what condition of man he considered the most pitiable: A lonesome man on a rainy day who does not know how to read.

➤ Tis a common observation here that our cause is the cause of all mankind, and that we are fighting for their liberty in defending our own.

➤ Sloth makes all things difficult, but industry all things easy.

➤ Hear reason, or she'll make you feel her.

➤ Those disputing, contradicting, and confuting people are generally unfortunate in their affairs. They get victory, sometimes, but they never get good will, which would be of more use to them.

➤ Order - Let all your things have their places; let each part of your business have its time.

➤ Be not sick too late, nor well too soon

- ➢ Avarice and Happiness never saw each other, how then should they become acquainted?

- ➢ Wine is constant proof that God loves us and loves to see us happy.

- ➢ Money never made a man happy yet, nor will it. There is nothing in its nature to produce happiness. The more a man has, the more he wants. Instead of its filling a vacuum, it makes one. If it satisfies one want, it doubles and trebles that want another way. That was a true proverb of the wise man, rely upon it; Better is little with the fear of the Lord, than great treasure, and trouble therewith.

- ➢ A word to the wise is enough, and many words won't fill a bushel.

- ➢ Chess teaches foresight, by having to plan ahead; vigilance, by having to keep watch over the whole chess board; caution, by having to restrain ourselves from making hasty moves; and finally, we learn from chess the greatest maxim in life - that even when everything seems to be going badly for us we should not lose heart, but always hoping for a change for the better, steadfastly continue searching for the solutions to our problems.

➢ Most people return small favors, acknowledge medium ones and repay greater ones - with ingratitude.

➢ Be neither silly, nor cunning, but wise

➢ Some are weatherwise, some are otherwise.

➢ Religion I found to be without any tendency to inspire, promote, or confirm morality, serves principally to divide us and make us unfriendly to one another.

➢ God works wonders now and then; Behold a lawyer, an honest man.

➢ We must not in the course of public life expect immediate approbation and immediate grateful acknowledgment of our services. But let us persevere through abuse and even injury. The internal satisfaction of a good conscience is always present, and time will do us justice in the minds of the people, even those at present the most prejudiced against us.

➢ There are two ways of being happy: We must
either diminish our wants or augment our
means - either may do - the result is the same
and it is for each man to decide for himself and
to do that which happens to be easier.

➢ A Man of Knowledge like a rich Soil, feeds If not
a world of Corn, a world of Weeds.

➢ Opportunity is the great bawd.

➢ An undutiful daughter will prove an
unmanageable wife.

➢ Why should I give my Readers bad lines of my
own when good ones of other People's are so
plenty?

➢ He that hath a Trade, hath an Estate.

➢ A little neglect may breed great mischief.

➢ Creditors are a superstitious sect, great
observers of set days and times.

➢ Trusting too much to others care is the ruin of
many.

- ➢ For Age and Want save while you may; No morning Sun lasts a whole day.

- ➢ Diligence overcomes difficulties; sloth makes them.

- ➢ Honesty is the best policy.

- ➢ As we must account for every idle word, so must we account for every idle silence.

- ➢ Those who give up their liberty for more security neither deserve liberty nor security.

- ➢ To be thrown upon one's own resources, is to be cast in the very lap of fortune.

- ➢ Nothing is so tiresome to one's self, as well as so odious to others, as disguise and affectation.

- ➢ The eye of the master will do more work than both his hands.

- ➢ Pain wastes the Body, Pleasures the Understanding.

- ➢ Rich widows are the only secondhand goods that sell at first-class prices.

- ➢ Many people die at twenty five and aren't buried until they are seventy five.

- ➢ Watch the pennies and the dollars will take care of themselves.

- ➢ Bad gains are true losses.

- ➢ Pay what you owe and you'll know what's your own.

- ➢ It is foolish to lay out money for the purchase of repentance.

- ➢ To bear other people's afflictions, everyone has courage and enough to spare.

- ➢ He that spends a Groat a day idly, spends idly above 6 l. a year, which is the Price of using 100 l.

- ➢ Beware the hobby that eats.

- ➢ For the best return on your money, pour your purse into your head.

➢ A man is sometimes more generous when he has but a little money than when he has plenty, perhaps through fear of being thought to have but little.

➢ They who have nothing to trouble them, will be troubled at nothing.

➢ He that hath a trade hath an estate; and he that hath a calling hath a place of profit and honor. A ploughman on his legs is higher than a gentleman on his knees.

➢ If we look back into history for the character of the present sects in Christianity, we shall find few that have not in their turns been persecutors, and complainers of persecution. The primitive Christians thought persecution extremely wrong in the Pagans, but practised it on one another.

➢ Indeed the general natural Tendency of Reading good History, must be, to fix in the Minds of Youth deep Impressions of the Beauty and Usefulness of Virtue of all Kinds, Publick Spirit, Fortitude.

➢ Anger and folly walk cheeck by jowl.

➤ Trouble springs from idleness, and grievous toil from needless ease.

➤ Idleness is the Dead Sea that swallows all virtues

➤ He that drinks his Cyder alone, let him catch his Horse alone.

➤ An Egg to day is better than a Hen to-morrow.

➤ He who is in love with himself has no rivals.

➤ Wink at small faults; remember thou hast great ones.

➤ A Republic, if you can keep it.

➤ I believe there is one Supreme most perfect being.

➤ Experience keeps a dear school, but fools will learn in no other.

➤ If time be of all things the most precious, wasting time must be the greatest prodigality.

➢ Did not strong connections draw me elsewhere, I believe Scotland would be the country I would choose to end my days in.

➢ Having been poor is no shame, but being ashamed of it, is.

➢ Nothing brings more pain than too much pleasure; nothing more bondage than too much liberty.

➢ There was never a good war, or a bad peace.

➢ We are spirits. That bodies should be lent us while they afford us pleasure, assist us in acquiring knowledge or in doing good to our fellow-creatures, is a kind of benevolent act of God. When they become unfit for these purposes and afford us pain instead of pleasure, instead of an aid become an encumbrance and answer none of these intentions for which they were given, it is equally kind and benevolent that a way is provided by which we get rid of them. Death is that way.

➢ I made the greater progress, from that clearness of head and quicker apprehension which generally attend temperance in eating and drinking.

➤ Would you live with ease, Do what you ought, and not what you please.

➤ Passion governs, and she never governs wisely.

➤ Nine Men in Ten are Suicides.

➤ Distrust and caution are the parents of security.

➤ Great talkers should be cropt, for they've no need of ears.

➤ Men are subject to various inconveniences merely through lack of a small share of courage, which is a quality very necessary in the common occurrences of life, as well as in a battle. How many impertinences do we daily suffer with great uneasiness, because we have not courage enough to discover our dislike.

➤ Use no hurtful deceit; think innocently and justly and, if you speak, speak accordingly.

➢ If all printers were determined not to print anything till they were sure it would offend nobody, there would be very little printed.

➢ Idleness and pride tax with a heavier hand than kings and governments.

➢ Setting too good an Example is a Kind of slander seldom forgiven.

➢ The church, the state, and the poor, are 3 daughters which we should maintain, but not portion off.

➢ All wars are follies, very expensive and very mischievous ones.

➢ Poverty often deprives a man of all spirit and virtue; it is hard for an empty bag to stand upright.

➢ Lend money to an enemy, and thou will gain him, to a friend and thou will lose him.

➢ Suspicion may be no fault, but showing it may be a great one.

- When will mankind be convinced and agree to settle their difficulties by arbitration?

- Hear no ill of a friend, nor speak any of an enemy.

- Hot things, sharp things, sweet things, cold things All rot the teeth, and make them look like old things.

- Cold & cunning come from the north: But cunning sans wisdom is nothing worth.

- Early to bed and early to rise, makes a man healthy, wealthy and wise." He planned his routine around waking up at 5 a.m. and asking himself "What good shall I do this day?

- What is best for people is what they do for themselves.

- Where there's no law, there's no bread.

- Cunning proceeds from want of capacity.

- If we do not hang together, we shall surely hang separately.

➢ If you, do what you should not, you must bear what you would not.

➢ After crosses and losses men grow humbler and wiser.

➢ No nation was ever ruined by trade.

➢ In order for three people to keep a secret, two must be dead.

➢ I think vital religion has always suffered when orthodoxy is more regarded than virtue. The scriptures assure me that at the last day we shall not be examined on what we thought but what we did.

➢ We may give advice, but we cannot give conduct.

➢ When women cease to be handsome, they study to be good.

➢ A great empire, like a great cake, is most easily diminished at the edges.

➢ The worst wheel of the cart makes the most noise.

- ➤ As often as we do good, we sacrifice.

- ➤ Think What You Do When You Run in Debt: You Give to Another Power over Your Liberty

- ➤ Men and Melons are hard to know.

- ➤ Love, Cough, & a Smoke, can't well be hid.

- ➤ To whom you betray your secret you sell your liberty.

- ➤ Genius without education is like silver in the mine.

- ➤ Strangers are welcome because there is room enough for them all, and therefore the old Inhabitants are not jealous of them; the Laws protect them sufficiently so that they have no need of the Patronage of great Men; and every one will enjoy securely the Profits of his Industry. But if he does not bring a Fortune with him, he must work and be industrious to live.

- ➤ Time is money.

- Three things are men most likely to be cheated in, a horse, a wig, and a wife.

- It is the man and woman united that makes the complete human being. Separate she lacks his force of body and strength of reason; he her softness, sensibility and acute discernment. Together they are most likely to succeed in the world.

- If you wouldn't live long, live well; for folly and wickedness shorten life.

- Life with Fools consists in Drinking; with the wise Man, living's Thinking.

- The foundation of all happiness in thinking rightly.

- Forewarn'd, forearm'd.

- When a religion is good, I conceive it will support itself; and when it does not support itself, and God does not take care to support it so that its professors are obliged to call for help of the civil power, 'tis a sign, I apprehend, of its being a bad one.

➢ If you want to be loved, love and be loveable.

➢ What is the use of a new-born child ?

➢ Little rogues easily become great ones.

➢ The people heard it, and approved the doctrine, and immediately practiced the contrary.

➢ There cannot be good living where there is not good drinking.

➢ The ancients tell us what is best; but we must learn of the moderns what is fittest.

➢ When Wine enters, out goes the Truth.

➢ He that hath a calling, hath an office of profit and honor.

➢ This modesty in a sect is perhaps a singular instance in the history of mankind, every other sect supposing itself in possession of all truth, and that those who differ are so far in the wrong ; like a man traveling in foggy weather, those at some distance before him on the road he sees wrapped up in the fog, as well as those behind him, and also the people in the fields on each side, but near him all appears clear, tho' in truth he is as much in the fog as any of them.

> Lost time can never be found again

> Love well, whip well.

> A countryman between two lawyers is like a fish between two cats.

> Vicious actions are not hurtful because they are forbidden, but forbidden because they are hurtful.

> In short, I conceive that great part of the miseries of mankind are brought upon them by the false estimates they have made of the value of things, and by their giving too much for their whistles.

> Experience keeps a dear school, but fools will learn in no other, and scarce in that; for it is true we may give advice, but we cannot give conduct.

> Little strokes fell great oaks.

➢ Let honesty be as the breath of thy soul; then shalt thou reach the point of happiness, and independence shall be thy shield and buckler, thy helmet and crown; then shall thy soul walk upright, nor stoop to the silken wretch because he hath riches, nor pocket an abuse because the hand which offers it wears a ring set with diamonds.

➢ If you'd be beloved, make yourself amiable. A true friend is the best possession.

➢ He that takes a wife, takes care

➢ Diligence is the mother of good luck, and God gives all things to industry. Work while it is called today, for you know not how much you may be hindered by tomorrow. One today is worth two tomorrows; never leave that till tomorrow which you can do to-day.

➢ When men are employed they are best contented.

➢ There is always room for the man of force.

➢ Great talkers are little doers.

➢ Those Who Sacrifice Liberty For Security Deserve Neither.

➢ History will also give occasion to expatiate on the advantage of civil orders and constitutions; how men and their properties are protected by joining in societies and establishing government; their industry encouraged and rewarded, arts invented, and life made more comfortable; the advantages of liberty, mischiefs of licentiousness, benefits arising from good laws and a due execution of justice. Thus may the first principles of sound politics be fixed in the minds of youth.

➢ Lost time is never found again, and what we call time enough, always proves little enough.

➢ I hope...that mankind will at length, as they call themselves reasonable creatures, have reason and sense enough to settle their differences without cutting throats; for in my opinion there never was a good war, or a bad peace.

➢ Take Courage, Mortal; Death can't banish thee out of the Universe.

➢ Since I cannot govern my own tongue, though within my own teeth, how can I hope to govern the tongue of others?

➢ There seems to be three ways for a nation to acquire wealth: the first is by war...this is robbery; the second by commerce, which is generally cheating; the third by agriculture, the only honest way.

➢ The proud hate pride in others.

➢ The refusal of King George to allow the colonies to operate an honest money system, which freed the ordinary man from clutches of the money manipulators was probably the prime cause of the revolution.

➢ We must, indeed, all hang together or, most assuredly, we shall all hang separately.

➢ A change of fortune hurts a wise man no more than a change of the moon.

➢ Thinking aloud is a habit which is responsible for most of mankind's misery.

- To get the bad customs of a country changed and new ones, though better, introduced, it is necessary first to remove the prejudices of the people, enlighten their ignorance, and convince them that their interests will be promoted by the proposed changes; and this is not the work of a day.

- If time be of all things the most precious, wasting time must be, as Poor Richard says, "the greatest prodigality'; since, as he elsewhere tells us, 'Lost time is never found again'; and 'What we call time enough always proves little enough'. Let us then up and be doing, and doing to the purpose; so by diligence shall we do more with less perplexity.

- By failing to prepare, you are preparing to fail.

- There are lazy minds as well as lazy bodies.

- It is only when the rich are sick that they fully feel the impotence of wealth.

- Before you consult your fancy, consult your purse.

- ➤ Human felicity is produced not as much by great pieces of good fortune that seldom happen as by little advantages that occur every day.

- ➤ Take it from Richard, poor and lame, What's begun in anger ends in shame.

- ➤ A highwayman is as much a robber when he plunders in a gang as when single; and a nation that makes an unjust war is only a great gang.

- ➤ Doing an injury puts you below your enemy; revenging one make you but even with him; forgiving it sets you above him.

- ➤ The longer I live the more convinced I become that God governs in the affairs of men. And have we now forgotten that powerful friend? Or do we imagine we no longer need His assistance.

- ➤ Wine is constant proof that God loves us and likes to see us happy.

- ➤ And where is the Prince who can afford to so cover his country with troops for its defense, as that ten thousand men descending from the clouds, might not in many places do an infinite deal of mischief, before a force could be brought together to repel them?

➢ We hear of the conversion of water into wine at the marriage in Cana as of a miracle. But this conversion is, through the goodness of God, made every day before our eyes. Behold the rain which descends from heaven upon our vineyards, and which incorporates itself with the grapes, to be changed into wine; a constant proof that God loves us, and loves to see us happy.

➢ A man can be beautiful physically, mentally, or personality wise. True beauty, though, is in the spirit. A genuine man who understands right and wrong, with a strong sense of self is beautiful. A man who can be compassionate and caring, but firm and wise. Someone who can do the right thing no matter who's around to see it. Even if the deed is unseen and unrecognized. That is a beautiful man. One today is worth two tomorrows.

➢ I have found Christian dogma unintelligible.

➢ Some volumes against Deism fell into my hands ... they produced an effect precisely the reverse to what was intended by the writers; for the arguments of the Deists, which were cited in order to be refuted, appeared to me much more forcibly than the refutation itself; in a word, I soon became a thorough Deist.

➢ Be not disturbed at trifles, or at accidents common or unavoidable.

➢ It would be thought a hard government that should tax its people one tenth part.

➢ If you give up your freedom for safety, you don't deserve either one

➢ The used key is always bright.

➢ The US Constitution only guarantees your rights as a citizen, it doesn't guarantee happiness. It may take work, but if you have your rights, happiness is very possible.

➢ The handshake of the host affects the taste of the roast

➢ If you desire many things, many things will seem few.

- The moral and religious system which Jesus Christ transmitted to us is the best the world has ever seen, or can see.

- Beauty and folly are old companions.

- In general, mankind, since the improvement of cookery, eats twice as much as nature requires.

- He that waits upon fortune, is never sure of a dinner.

- A life of leisure and a life of laziness are two things. There will be sleeping enough in the grave.

- He that raises a large family does, indeed, while he lives to observe them, stand a broader mark for sorrow; but then he stands a broader mark for pleasure too.

- There will be plenty of time to sleep once you are dead

- Drive thy business or it will drive thee.

- Even peace may be purchased at too high a price.

➢ Death is a fisherman, the world we see His fish-pond is, and we the fishes be; His net some general sickness; howe'er he Is not so kind as other fishers be; For if they take one of the smaller fry, They throw him in again, he shall not die: But death is sure to kill all he can get, And all is fish with him that comes to net.

➢ I should have no objection to go over the same life from its beginning to the end: requesting only the advantage authors have, of correcting in a second edition the faults of the first.

➢ If we give up freedom for security, we are in danger of losing both.

➢ Let thy vices die before thee.

➢ Courteous Reader, Astrology is one of the most ancient Sciences, held in high esteem of old, by the Wise and the Great. Formerly, no Prince would make War or Peace, nor any General fight in Battle, in short, no important affair was undertaken without first consulting an Astrologer.

➢ He's a fool that makes his doctor his heir.

➢ Success has ruin'd many a man.

➢ Industry and patience are the surest means of plenty.

➢ Ambition has its disappointments to sour us, but never the good fortune to satisfy us. Its appetite grows keener by indulgence and all we can gratify it with at present serves but the more to inflame its insatiable desires.

➢ Make the best use of both time and money. Add industry and frugal dealings if they pay very well and if you're free to it.

➢ The wise man draws more advantage from his enemies than the fool from his friends

➢ Those who are willing to forfeit liberty for security will have neither.

➢ Governments having failed the people, the people are entirely justified in assuming for themselves an essential role in government. Where a government takes proper measures to protect the people under its care, such a proceeding might have been thought both unnecessary and unjustifiable: But here it is quite the Reverse.

➢ Do not fear mistakes.

➢ Friends and neighbors complain that taxes are indeed very heavy, and if those laid on by the government were the only ones we had to pay, we might the more easily discharge them; but we have many others, and much more grievous to some of us. We are taxed twice as much by our idleness, three times as much by our pride, and four times as much by our folly.

➢ There is none deceived but he that trusts.

➢ The good will of the governed will be starved if not fed by the good deeds of the governors.

➢ Neglect mending a small fault and 'twill soon be a great one.

➢ It is observable that God has often called men to places of dignity and honor when they have been busy in the honest employment of their vocation.

- A spoonful of honey will catch more flies than a gallon of vinegar.

- When nature gave us tears, She gave us leave to weep.

- The greatest monarch on the proudest throne is obliged to sit upon his own arse.

- The first Degree of Folly, is to conceit one's self wise; the second to profess it; the third to despise Counsel.

- If you'd lose a troublesome visitor, lend him money.

- A flatterer never seems absurd: The flatter'd always takes his word.

- Rules too soft are seldomly followed; rules too harsh are seldomly executed.

- Cut the Wings of your Hens and Hopes, lest they lead you a weary Dance after them.

- E'er you remark another's sin, bid your own conscience look within.

➢ Display is as false as it is costly.

➢ He's gone, and forgot nothing but to say farewell to his creditors

➢ When you taste honey, remember gall.

➢ Eyes and Priests Bear no Jests.

➢ If you want a neat wife, choose her on a Saturday.

➢ How can any Action be meritorious of Praise or Dispraise, Reward or Punishment, when the natural Principle of Self-Love is the only and the irresistible Motive to it?

➢ He that pays for work before it's done, has but a pennyworth for two pence.

➢ While the path to wealth is clearly marked, few are willing to adapt themselves to the modest discipline that the journey requires. Instead, most choose the shinier track of debt-driven consumption, which they find further along is covered in vines and thorns.

➢ You don't get somebody to like you by doing them a favor. That only tends to build resentment over the fact that they are needy and you are not. No, you ask them to do you a favor.

➢ Contentment makes a poor person rich and discontent makes a rich person poor.

➢ Trouble Springs From Idleness.

➢ Vice knows [its] ugly, so [it] puts on [a] mask.

➢ Marry above thy match and you will get a master.

➢ Would thou confound thy enemy, be good thyself.

➢ A penny saved is twopence dear; A pin a day 's a groat a year.

➢ Neither a Fortress nor a Maidenhead will hold out long after they begin to parley.

➢ The Difficulty lies, in finding out an exact Measure but eat for Necessity, not Pleasure, for Lust knows not where Necessity ends.

- ➢ The King's cheese is half wasted in parings: But no matter, 'tis made of the people's milk.

- ➢ Hope is an essential constituent of human life.

- ➢ Blessed is he that expects nothing, for he shall never be disappointed. expect nothing - get nothing! but expect something - get something!!

- ➢ Hope of gain lessens pain.

- ➢ Constant dropping wears away stones

- ➢ A man may, if he knows not how to save as he gets, keep his nose to the grindstone.

- ➢ Force shites upon Reason's Back.

- ➢ One mend-fault is worth two find-faults, but one find-fault is better than two make-faults.

- ➢ Content and Riches seldom meet together, Riches take thou, contentment I had rather.

- ➢ Keep flax from fire, and youth from gaming.

> You will discover 3 trustworthy mates, an aged wife, an aged canine, and ready dollars.

> He is no clown that drives the plow, but he that doth clownish things.

> Don't think so much of your own Cunning, as to forget other Men's; a Cunning Man is overmatched by a cunning Man and a Half.

> Proclaim not all though knowest, or all though owest.

> I wish it were possible, from this instance, to invent a method of embalming drowned persons in such a manner that they may be recalled to life at any period, however distant; for having a very ardent desire to see and observe the state of America a hundred years hence, I should prefer to any ordinary death the being immersed in a cask of Madeira wine with a few friends till that time, to be then recalled to life by the solar warmth of my dear country!

> Get what you can, and what you get hold; 'tis the Stone that will turn all your Lead into Gold.

- Kings have long arms, but Misfortune longer: let none think themselves out of her reach.

- When you assemble a number of men to have the advantage of their joint wisdom, you inevitably assemble with those men all their prejudices, their passions, their errors of opinion, their local interests and their selfish views.

- Unless the Stream of their Importation could be turned... they will soon so outnumber us, that all the advantages we have, will not in my Opinion be able to preserve our Language, and even our Government will become precarious.

- For over 1,700 years, the Jews have been bewailing their sad fate in that they have been exiled from their homeland, as they call Palestine. But gentlemen, did the world give it to them in fee simple, they would at once find some reason for not returning. Why? Because they are vampires, and vampires do not live on vampires. They cannot live only among themselves. They must subsist on Christians and other people not of their race.

- He that's secure is not safe.

- Sarcasm is the lowest form of humor but the highest form of flattery.

- Proclaim not all thou knowest, all thou knowest, all thou hast, nor all thou cans't.

- A perfect character might be attended with the inconvenience of being envied and hated; and that a benevolent man should allow a few faults in himself, to keep his friends in countenance.

- He that lieth down with Dogs, shall rise up with Fleas.

- Praise to the undeserving is severe satire.

- Fools make feasts and wise men eat them.

- Never spare the parson's wine nor the baker's pudding

- Many dishes many diseases, Many medicines few cures.

- To be proud of knowledge is to be blind with light.

- ➢ Take heed of the Vinegar of sweet Wine, and the Anger of Good-nature.

- ➢ Be temperate in wine, in eating, girls, & sloth; Or the Gout will seize you and plague you both.

- ➢ Ill customs and bad advice are seldom forgotten.

- ➢ Don't think to hunt two hares with one dog.

- ➢ A lighthouse is more useful than a church.

- ➢ If thou hast wit and learning, add to it wisdom and modesty.

- ➢ All things are cheap to the saving, dear to the wasteful

- ➢ ...it is prodigious the quantity of good that may be done by one man if he will make a business of it.

- ➢ There is nothing so absurd as knowledge spun too fine.

- ➢ He'll cheat without scruple, who can without fear.

➢ The way to see by faith is to shut the eye of reason: The Morning Daylight appears plainer when you put out your Candle.

➢ Great good nature without prudence is a great misfortune.

➢ Tomorrow, every Fault is to be amended; but that Tomorrow never comes.

➢ A true friend is the greatest possesion.

➢ They that will not be counseled, cannot be helped. If you do not hear reason she will rap you on the knuckles.

➢ There is no such thing as a good war or a bad peace.

➢ If I knew a miser, who gave up every kind of comfortable living, all the pleasure of doing good to others, all the esteem of his fellow-citizens, and the joys of benevolent friendship, for the sake of accumulating wealth. Poor man, said I, you pay too much for your whistle.

➢ Much Virtue in Herbs, little in Men.

➢ The Sting of a reproach, is the Truth of it.

➢ Remember, that money is of the prolific, generating nature. Money can beget money, and its offspring can beget more, and so on. Five shillings turned is six, turned again it is seven and threepence, and so on, till it becomes a hundred pounds. The more there is of it, the more it produces every turning, so that the profits rise quicker and quicker. He that kills a breeding sow, destroys all her offspring to the thousandth generation. He that murders a crown, destroys all that it might have produced, even scores of pounds.

➢ I imagine it great vanity in me to suppose that the Supremely Perfect does in the least regard such an inconsiderable nothing as man. More especially, since it is impossible for me to have any positive, clear idea of that which is infinite and incomprehensible, I cannot conceive otherwise than that He, the Infinite Father, expects or requires no worship or praise from us, but that He is even infinitely above it.

➢ Temperance... drink not to elevation. (2) Silence... avoid trifling conversations. (3) Order:

Let all your things have their places... (4)
Resolution... perform without fail what you
resolve. (5) Frugality... i.e. waste nothing. (6)
Industry: Lose no time; be always employ'd... (7)
Sincerity: Use no hurtful deceit; think
innocently... (8) Justice: Wrong none by doing
injuries... (9) Moderation: Avoid extremes;
forbear resenting... (10) Cleanliness: Tolerate no
uncleanliness in body... (11) Tranquility: Be not
disturbed at trifles... (12) Chastity (13) Humility :
Imitate Jesus.

➤ He that lives upon hope will die fasting.

➤ If you have a secret and tell someone everyone
will know. You can only keep a secret if you
don't tell anyone.

➤ Approve not of him who commends all you say.

➤ Applause waits on success.

➤ Tis easy to see, hard to foresee.

➤ When you are finished changing, you are
finished.

➤ Virtue and Happiness are Mother and Daughter.

➢ Our Constitution is in actual operation; everything appears to promise that it will last; but in this world nothing is certain but death and taxes.

➢ Want of care does us more damage than want of knowledge

➢ The most acceptable service of God is doing good to man.

➢ Let no pleasure tempt thee, no profit allure thee, no persuasion move thee, to do anything which thou knowest to be evil; so shalt thou always live jollity; for a good conscience is a continual Christmas.

➢ Hold your Council before Dinner; the full Belly hates Thinking as well as Acting.

➢ Most fools think they are only ignorant.

➢ Learn of the skillful; he that teaches himself, has a fool for his master.

➢ One today is worth two tomorrows.

> If you have a bald head don't walk out in the sun because you will get burned.

> One of the advantages of being a 'reasonable creature' is that one can find a reason for whatever one wants to do.

> Be in general virtuous, and you will be happy.

> Pride breakfasted with plenty, dined with poverty, and supped with infamy.

> The art of acting consists in keeping people from coughing.

> Wealth is not his that has it, but his that enjoys it.

> He that rises late must trot all day.

> Life is a kind of Chess, with struggle, competition, good and ill events.

> Success has ruined many a man.

> Do you love truth for truth's sake, and will you endeavor impartially to find and receive it yourself, and communicate it to others?

➢ Speak with contempt of none, from slave to king, The meanest Bee hath, and will use, a sting.

➢ Do you love life? Then don't waste time, because time is life!

➢ To Follow by faith alone is to follow blindly.

➢ A man compounded of law and gospel is able to cheat a whole country with his religion and then destroy them under color of law

➢ A full Belly is the Mother of all Evil.

➢ Blame-all and Praise-all are two blockheads.

➢ Two dry Sticks will burn a green One.

➢ The sleeping fox catches no poultry.

➢ Why does the blind man's wife paint herself.

➢ He that would travel much, should eat little.

➢ Many have quarreled about religion that never practice it.

➤ Strict punctuality is a cheap virtue.

➤ Innocence is its own defense.

➤ Men take more pains to mask than mend.

➤ In success be moderate.

➤ No man ought to own more property than needed for his livelihood; the rest, by right, belonged to the state.

➤ He who falls in love with himself will have no rivals.

➤ Private property ... is a Creature of Society, and is subject to the Calls of that Society, whenever its Necessities shall require it, even to its last Farthing, its contributors therefore to the public Exigencies are not to be considered a Benefit on the Public, entitling the Contributors to the Distinctions of Honor and Power, but as the Return of an Obligation previously received, or as payment for a just Debt.

➤ He does not possess wealth; it possesses him.

- ➢ The next thing most like living one's life over again seems to be a recollection of that life, and to make that recollection as durable as possible by putting it down in writing.

- ➢ As we benefit from the inventions of others, we should be glad to share our own ... freely and gladly.

- ➢ My rule, in which I have always found satisfaction, is, never to turn aside in public affairs through views of private interest; but to go straight forward in doing what appears to me right at the time, leaving the consequences with Providence.

- ➢ The things which hurt, instruct.

- ➢ One Man may be more cunning than another, but not more cunning than every body else.

- ➢ If any form of government is capable of making a nation happy, ours I think bids fair now for producing that effect. But after all much depends upon the people who are governed.

- ➢ Without industry and frugality, nothing will do; with them, everything.

➢ Great spenders are bad lenders.

➢ Fear to do ill, and you need fear else.

➢ If you ever need a helping hand, you'll find one at the end of your arm. Beer is living proof that God loves us and wants to see us happy.

➢ The key that unlocks a door is a key to keep if you want to go through that door again.

➢ A full Belly makes a dull Brain: The Muses starve in a Cook's Shop.

➢ You may sometimes be much in the Wrong, in owning your being in the Right.

➢ Where security exists, liberty and opportunity do not.

➢ Vice knows she is ugly, so puts on her mask.

➢ Grievances cannot be redressed until they are known; and they cannot be known but through complaints and petitions. If these are deemed affronts, and the messengers punished as offenders, who will henceforth send petitions?

And who will deliver them? Wise governments encouraged the airing of grievances, even those that were lightly founded Foolish governments did the opposite - to their peril. Where complaining is a crime, hope becomes despair.

> He that would fish, must venture his bait.

> Let honesty and industry be thy constant companions, and spend one penny less than thy clear gains; then shall thy pocket begin to thrive; creditors will not insult, nor want oppress, nor hungerness bite, nor nakedness freeze thee

> The poor man must walk to get meat for his stomach, the rich man to get a stomach to his meat.

> What is the recipe for successful achievement? Choose a career you love. Give it the best there is in you. Seize your opportunities. And be a member of the team.

> If we are industrious, we shall never starve; for, at the workingman's house hunger looks in, but dares not enter. Nor will the bailiff or the

constable enter, for industry pays debts, while despair increaseth them.

➢ It is much easier to suppress a first desire than to satisfy those that follow.

➢ Teach your child to hold his tongue; he'll learn fast enough to speak.

➢ Can anything be constant in a world which is eternally changing?

➢ Bargaining has neither friends nor relations.

➢ I resolve to speak ill of no man whatever, not even in a matter of truth; but rather by some means excuse the faults I hear charged upon others, and upon proper occasions speak all the good I know of everybody.

➢ I wish it (Christianity) were more productive of good works ... I mean real good works ... not holy day keeping, sermon-hearing ... or making long prayers, filled with flatteries and compliments despised by wise men, and much less capable of pleasing the Deity.

➢ Where liberty is, there is my country.

➢ God heals, and the doctor takes the fees. Energy and persistence conquer all things. He that is good for making excuses is seldom good for anything else. How many observe Christ's birthday! How few, his precepts! Oh, it's easier to keep Holidays than Commandments. Well done is better than well said.

➢ Money is of a prolific generating nature. Money can beget money, and its offspring can beget more.

➢ I early found that when I worked for myself alone, myself alone worked for me; but when I worked for others also, others worked also for me.

➢ Righteousness, or justice, is, undoubtedly of all the virtues, the surest foundation on which to create and establish a new state. But there are two nobler virtues, industry and frugality, which tend more to increase the wealth, power and grandeur of the community, than all the others without them.

➢ It is the will of God and Nature that these mortal bodies be laid aside, when the soul is to enter into real life; 'tis rather an embrio state, a preparation for living; a man is not completely born until he be dead: Why then should we grieve that a new child is born among the immortals?

➢ Women are books, and men the readers be, Who sometimes in those books erratas see; Yet oft the reader's raptured with each line, Fair print and paper, fraught with sense divine; Tho' some, neglectful, seldom care to read, And faithful wives no more than bibles heed. Are women books? says Hodge, then would mine were An Almanack, to change her every year.

➢ In short, the way to wealth, if you desire it, is as plain as the way to market. It depends chiefly on two works, industry and frugality.

➢ Prodigality of Time produces Poverty of Mind as well as of Estate.

➢ I saw few die of hunger; of eating, a hundred thousand.

➢ Keep thy shop, and thy shop will keep thee.

➢ Patience in Market, is worth Pounds in a year.

➢ I am a mortal enemy to arbitrary government and unlimited power.

➢ Who is rich? He that is content. Who is that? Nobody.

➢ I would rather have it said, 'He lived usefully,' than, 'He died rich.'

➢ The United States Constitutional Convention, except for three or four persons, thought prayers unnecessary.

➢ In prosperous fortunes be modest and wise, The greatest may fall, and the lowest may rise: But insolent People that fall in disgrace, Are wretched and nobody pities their Case.

➢ I cannot conceive otherwise than that He, the Infinite Father, expects or requires no worship or praise from us, but that He is even infinitely above it.

➢ Do well by doing good.

- The two most beautiful sights I have witnessed in my life are a full blown ship at sail and the round-bellied pregnant female.

- Those who would give up liberty for safety deserve neither.

- I think opinions should be judged by their influences and effects; and if a man holds none that tend to make him less virtuous or more vicious, it may be concluded that he holds none that are dangerous, which I hope is the case with me.

- Games lubricate the body and the mind.

- He who gives up freedom for safety deserves neither.

- America cultivates best what Germany brought forth.

- Who pleasure gives, Shall joy receive

- Chess is so interesting in itself, as not to need the view of gain to induce engaging in it; and thence it is never played for money

➢ La pereza anda tan despacio que la pobreza no tarda en alcanzarla.

➢ Finding myself to exist in the world, I believe I shall, in some shape or other, always exist.

➢ Those who would trade in their freedom for their protection deserve neither.

➢ He that drinks fast, pays slow.

➢ Taxes are indeed very heavy - We are taxed twice as much by our Idleness. Three times as much by our Pride. And four times as much by our Folly.

➢ The discovery of a wine is of greater moment than the discovery of a constellation. The universe is too full of stars.

➢ Those who give up liberty for the sake of security, deserve neither liberty nor security.

➢ If a man empties his purse into his head, no one can take it from him.

➤ Dangerous, therefore, is it to take shelter under a tree, during a thunder-gust. It has been fatal to many, both men and beasts.

➤ You can bear your own faults, and why not a fault in your wife?

➤ Fear not death; for the sooner we die, the longer shall we be immortal.

➤ I was surprised to find myself so much fuller of Faults than I had imagined, but I had the Satisfaction of seeing them diminish.

➤ We are not so sensible of the greatest Health as of the least Sickness.

➤ It is a strange anomaly that men could be careful to insure their houses, their ships, their merchandise, and yet neglect to insure their lives - surely the most important of all to their families, and more subject to loss.

➤ Tis a great confidence in a friend to tell him your faults; greater to tell him his.

➤ I never turned to drink. It seemed to turn to me.

➢ To be proud of virtue, is to poison yourself with the Antidote.

➢ Handle your tools without mittens.

➢ Love your Neighbour; yet don't pull down your Hedge.

➢ Those have a short Lent who owe money to be paid at Easter.

➢ If we lose our Money, it gives us some Concern. If we are cheated or robb'd of it, we are angry: But Money lost may be found; what we are robb'd of may be restored: The Treasure of Time once lost, can never be recovered; yet we squander it as tho' 'twere nothing worth, or we had no Use for it.

➢ Leisure is the time for doing something useful. This leisure the diligent person will obtain the lazy one never.

➢ Take counsel in wine, but resolve afterwards in water.

➢ Wine makes daily living easier, less hurried with fewer tensions and more tolerance.

> ➤ Here comes the orator with his flood of words
and his drop of reason.

> ➤ I have conceived a higher opinion of the natural
capacities of the black race than I had ever
before entertained. Their apprehension seems
as quick, their memory as strong, and their
docility in every respect equal to that of white
children.

> ➤ The apostle Paul very seriously advised Timothy
to put some wine in his water for health's sake,
but not one of the apostles nor any of the holy
fathers have ever recommended putting water
in wine

> ➤ Truth and sincerity have a certain distinguishing
native lustre about them which cannot be
perfectly counterfeited; they are like fire and
flame, that cannot be painted.

> ➤ She laughs at everything you say. Why? Because
she has fine teeth.

> ➤ I wish the bald eagle had not been chosen as
the representative of our country; he is a bird of
bad moral character; like those among men

who live by sharping and robbing, he is generally poor, and often very lousy. The turkey is a much more respectable bird, and withal a true original native of America.

➢ There never was a good knife made of bad steel.

➢ Resolve to perform what you ought; perform without fail what you resolve.

➢ Most people die at 25 but are buried at 75.

➢ To all apparent beauties blind, each blemish strikes an envious mind.

➢ Where there's marriage without love, there will be love without marriage.

➢ I believe that Man is not the most perfect Being but One, rather that as there are many Degrees of Beings his Inferiors, so there are many Degrees of Beings superior to him.

➢ While we may not be able to control all that happens to us, we can control what happens inside us.

➢ A single man has not nearly the value he would have in a state of union. He is an incomplete animal. He resembles the odd half of a pair of scissors.

➢ All human situations have their inconveniences. We feel those of the present but neither see nor feel those of the future; and hence we often make troublesome changes without amendment, and frequently for the worse.

➢ If passion drives you, let reason hold the reins.

➢ There is no kind of dishonesty into which otherwise good people more easily and frequently fall than that of defrauding the government.

➢ Our necessities never equal our wants.

➢ Getting it done is my reward.

➢ Who judges best of a Man, his Enemies or himself?

➢ Interest which blinds some People, enlightens others.

➢ My father's little library consisted chiefly of books in polemic divinity, most of which I read, and have since often regretted that, at a time when I had such a thirst for knowledge, more proper books had not fallen in my way since it was now resolved I should not be a clergyman.

➢ It is a grand mistake to think of being great without goodness and I pronounce it as certain that there was never a truly great man that was not at the same time truly virtuous.

➢ A new truth is a truth, an old error is an error.

➢ The good Education of Youth has been esteemed by wise Men in all Ages, as the surest Foundation of the Happiness both of private Families and of Common-wealths. Almost all Governments have therefore made it a principal Object of their Attention, to establish and endow with proper Revenues, such Seminaries of Learning, as might supply the succeeding Age with Men qualified to serve the Publick with Honour to themselves, and to their Country.

➢ Time is the stuff life is made of.

➢ Revealed religion has no weight with me.

➢ When confronted with two courses of action I jot down on a piece of paper all the arguments in favor of each one, then on the opposite side I write the arguments against each one. Then by weighing the arguments pro and con and cancelling them out, one against the other, I take the course indicated by what remains.

➢ An assembly of great men is the greatest fool upon earth.

➢ Taxes on consumption, like those on capital or income, to be just, must be uniform.

➢ It is much to be lamented that a man of Franklin's general good character and great influence should have been an unbeliever in Christianity, and also have done as much as he did to make others unbelievers.

➢ He that steals the old man's supper does him no wrong.

➢ Historians relate not so much what is done as what they would have believed.

➢ A virtuous heretic shall be saved before a wicked Christian.

➢ I am in the prime of senility.

➢ Venison and venery defeated me.

➢ It's the easiest thing in the world for a man to deceive himself.

➢ Do good to thy friend to keep him, to thy enemy to gain him.

➢ By heaven we understand a state of happiness infinite in degree, and endless in duration.

➢ No employment can be managed without arithmetic, no mechanical invention without geometry.

➢ He that can take rest is greater than he that can take cities.

➢ The expenses required to prevent a war are much lighter than those that will, if not prevented, be absolutely necessary to maintain it.

➢ When passion rules, she never rules wisely.

➢ Snowy winter, a plentiful harvest.

➢ Some men grow mad by studying much to know, But who grows mad by studying good to grow.

➢ Since they are our right, let us be vigilant to preserve them uninfringed, and free from encroachments. If animosities arise, and we should be obliged to resort to party, let each of us range himself on the side which unfurls the ensigns of public good. Faction will then vanish, which, if not timely suppressed, may overturn the balance, the palladium of liberty, and crush us under its ruins.

➢ Strive to be the best and you may succeed: he may well win the race that runs by himself.

➢ Would you persuade, speak of interest, not of reason.

➢ I look upon death to be as necessary to our constitution as sleep. We shall rise refreshed in the morning.

➢ Whoever feels pain in hearing a good character of his neighbor, will feel a pleasure in the reverse. And those who despair to rise in distinction by their virtues, are happy if others can be depressed to a level of themselves.

➢ It is ill-manners to silence a fool and cruelty to let him go on

➢ What good shall I do this day?

➢ Some of the domestic evils of drunkenness are houses without windows, gardens without fences, fields without tillage, barns without roofs, children without clothing, principles, morals or manners.

➢ We must hang together, gentlemen...else, we shall most assuredly hang separately.

➢ I know not which lives more unnatural lives, obeying husbands, or commanding wives.

➢ Mine is better than ours.

➢ Don't cry over spilled milk

➤ Many a long dispute among divines may be thus
abridged: It is so; It is not so. It is so; it is not so.

➤ Paintings and fightings are best seen at a
distance.

➤ Carelessness does more harm than a want of
knowledge.

➤ My List of Virtues contain'd at first but twelve:
But a Quaker Friend having kindly inform'd me
that I was generally thought proud; that my
Pride show'd itself frequently in Conversation;
that I was not content with being in the right
when discussing any Point, but was overbearing
& rather insolent; of which he convinc'd me by
mentioning several Instances; - I determined
endeavouring to cure myself ..., and I added
Humility to my List, giving an extensive Meaning
to the Word.

➤ Constant complaint is the poorest sort of pay
for all the comforts we enjoy.

➤ As Pride increases, Fortune declines.

➤ Virtue may not always make a Face handsome,
but Vice will certainly make it ugly.

➤ When Knaves betray each other, one can scarce be blamed or the other pitied.

➤ I think that humanity brings much misery on itself by the false value they put on things.

➤ Traveling is one way of lengthening life, at least in appearance.

➤ Oh the wonderful knowledge to be found in the stars. Even the smallest things are written there ... if you had but skill to read.

➤ If it were not for the Belly, the Back might wear Gold.

➤ When you're testing to see how deep water is, never use two feet.

➤ One today is worth two tomorrows. Lost time is never found again. Time is money. Dost thou love life? Then do not squander time, for that's the stuff that life is made of. You may delay, but time will not.

- ➢ Idleness and pride tax with a heavier hand than kings and parliaments. If we can get rid of the former, we may easily bear the latter.

- ➢ I believe in one God, Creator of the Universe in that He ought to be whipped from pilar to post and back again for His shameful actions toward Humanity.

- ➢ I have never seen the Philosopher's Stone that turns lead into Gold, but I have known the pursuit of it turn a Man's Gold into Lead.

- ➢ There are more old drunkards than old doctors.

- ➢ There have been as great souls unknown to fame as any of the most famous.

- ➢ Better slip with foot than tongue.

- ➢ In rivers and bad governments the lightest things swim at top.

- ➢ There are no ugly loves nor handsome prisons.

- ➢ Singularity in the right hath ruined many; happy those who are convinced of the general opinion.

➢ Nothing great comes without enthusiasm.

➢ What signifies knowing the Names, if you know not the Natures of things.

➢ I wish to live without committing any fault at any time.

➢ The thrifty maxim of the wary Dutch, Is to save all the Money they can touch

➢ Reader, I wish thee Health, Wealth, Happiness, And may kind Heaven thy Year's Industry bless.

➢ Is there anything men take more pains about than to render themselves unhappy?

➢ The misers cheese is wholesomest

➢ Revelation, indeed, as such had no influence on my mind

➢ A ploughman on his legs is higher than a gentleman on his knees.

➢ A little House well fill'd, a little Field well till'd, and a little Wife well will'd, are great Riches.

- An ounce of wit that is bought, Is worth a pound that is taught.

- He that sows Thorns, should never go barefoot.

- A temperate Diet frees from Diseases; such are seldom ill, but if they are surprised with Sickness, they bear it better, and recover sooner; for most Distempers have their Original from Repletion.

- Visit your Aunt, but not every Day; and call at your Brother's, but not every night.

- Evil, as evil, can never be chosen; and though evil is often the effect of our own choice, yet we never desire it but under the appearance of an imaginary good.

- Whether a Commonwealth suffers more by hypocritical pretenders to religion or by the openly profane? The most dangerous hypocrite in a Commonwealth is one who leaves the gospel for the sake of the law. A man compounded of law and gospel is able to cheat a whole country with his religion and then destroy them under color of law.

> Fiction or fable allures to instruction.

> All cats are gray in the dark.

> Many have been ruined by buying good Pennyworths.

> Pride is as loud a beggar as want, and a great deal more saucy. When you have bought one fine thing, you must buy ten more, that your appearance may be all of a piece; but it is easier to suppress the first desire than to satisfy all that follow it.

> Do not let fancy outrun your means.

> That man alone loves himself rightly who procures the greatest possible good to himself through the whole of his existence and so pursues pleasure as not to give for it more than it is worth.

> Stand firm, don't flutter!

> He gives twice that gives soon, i.e., he will soon be called to give again.

➢ Marry your son when you will, but you daughter
when you can.

➢ A nod from a lord is a breakfast for a fool.

➢ Justice is as strictly due between neighbor
nations as between neighbor citizens.

➢ If the elbow had been placed closer to the hand,
the forearm would have been too short to bring
the glass to the mouth; and if it had been closer
to the shoulder, the forearm would have been
so long that it would have carried the glass
beyond the mouth.

➢ Men's minds do not die with their bodies but
are made more happy or miserable after this
life according to their actions.

➢ Let our Fathers and Grandfathers be valued for
their Goodness, ourselves for our own.

➢ Let thy discontents be thy secrets; if the world
knows them 'twill despise thee and increase
them.

➢ All the heavenly Bodies, the Stars and Planets,
are regulated with the utmost Wisdom! And can

we suppose less Care to be taken in the Order
of the moral than in the natural System?

➢ Avoid dishonest gain: no price can recompence
the pangs of vice.

➢ It is therefore wish'd that all commerce were as
free between all the nations of the world as it is
between the several counties of England.

➢ If you ride a horse, sit close and tight, if you ride
a man, sit easy and light.

➢ A light purse is a heavy curse.

➢ Do you sincerely declare that you love mankind
in general, of what profession or religion
soever? Do you think any person ought to be
harmed in his body, name, or goods, for mere
speculative opinions, or his external way of
worship? Do you love truth for truth's sake; and
will you endeavor impartially to find and receive
it yourself, and communicate it to others.

➢ Abuses of the freedom of speech ought to be
repressed, but to whom are we to commit the
power of doing it?

➢ When the well is dry, people know the worth of water. [so appreciate what you have while you have it]

➢ If your head is made of wax, don't walk in the sun

➢ He [the Rev. Mr. Whitefield] used, indeed, sometimes to pray for my conversion, but never had the satisfaction of believing that his prayers were heard.

➢ If you can't pay for a thing, don't buy it. If you can't get paid for it, don't sell it.

➢ Mankind are very odd creatures: one half censure what they practice, the other half practice what they censure; the rest always say and do as they ought.

➢ Be not niggardly of what costs thee nothing, as courtesy, counsel, & countenance.

➢ A little sturdiness when superiors are much in the wrong sometimes occasions consideration. And there is truth in the old saying that if you make yourself a sheep, the wolves will eat you.

- Remember, Sir, that [England] began the slave trade!

- Now I've a sheep and a cow, every body bids me good morrow.

- In order to be happy you need a good dog, a good woman, and ready money.

- No man ever was glorious, who was not laborious.

- If any man flatters me, I'll flatter him again; tho' he were my best Friend.

- The cunning man steals a horse, the wise man lets him alone.

- No longer virtuous no longer free; is a Maxim as true with regard to a private Person as a Common-wealth.

- Graft good Fruit all, or graft not at all.

- A ship under sail and a big-bellied woman, Are the handsomest two things that can be seen common.

➢ Tis against some mens principle to pay interest, and seems against others interest to pay the principle.

➢ I consent Sir, to this Constitution because I expect no better, and because I am not sure, that it is not the best.

➢ Look round the habitable world, how few Know their own good, or, knowing it, pursue!

➢ Wherever desirable superfluities are imported, industry is excited, and thereby plenty is produced. Were only necessaries permitted to be purchased, men would work no more than was necessary for that purpose.

➢ If you would not be forgotten, do things worth remembering.

➢ Acquire Riches by Industry and Frugality.

➢ A place for everything, everything in its place.

➢ There is nothing wrong with retirement as long as one doesn't allow it to interfere with one's work.

> As charms are nonsense, nonsense is a charm.

> ... there is much truth in the Italian saying, 'Make yourselves sheep, and the wolves will eat you.'

> So convenient a thing to be a reasonable creature, since it enables one to find or make a reason for every thing one has a mind to do.

> You will see in this my notion of good works, that I am far from expecting to merit heaven by them. By heaven we understand a state of happiness, infinite in degree, and eternal in duration. I can do nothing to deserve such rewards... Even the mixed imperfect pleasures we enjoy in this world, are rather from God's goodness than our merit, how much more such happiness of heaven!

> We have been assured, Sir, in the Sacred Writings, that 'except the Lord build the House, they labor in vain that build it' I firmly believe this; by our partial local interests; our projects will be confounded, and we ourselves shall become a reproach and a by word down to future ages.

➢ The only certain things in life are death and taxes!

➢ On the whole, though I never arrived at the perfection I had been so ambitious of obtaining, but fell far short of it, yet I was, by the endeavor, a better and a happier man than I otherwise should have been had I not attempted it.

➢ I am about courting a girl I have had but little acquaintance with. How shall I come to a knowledge of her faults, and whether she has the virtues I imagine she has? Answer. Commend her among her female acquaintances.

➢ Slavery is such an atrocious debasement of human nature, that its very extirpation, if not performed with solicitous care, may sometimes open a source of serious evils.

➢ The grand leap of the whale up the Fall of Niagara is esteemed, by all who have seen it, as one of the finest spectacles in nature.

> Let me resolve to be virtuous, that I may be happy, that I may please Him, who is delighted to see me happy. Amen.

> The best way to help the poor is to make them uncomfortable in their own poverty.

> Then plough deep while sluggards sleep, and you shall have corn to sell and to keep.

> Despair ruins some, presumption many.

> Some make Conscience of wearing a Hat in the Church, who make none of robbing the Altar.

> There's no gain, without pain.

> I am the laziest man in the world. I invented all those things to save myself from toil.

> An apple a day keeps the doctor away.

> We are more thoroughly an enlightened people, with respect to our political interests, than perhaps any other under heaven. Every man among us reads, and is so easy in his circumstances as to have leisure for

conversations of improvement and for acquiring information.

➢ People who are willing to give up freedom for the sake of short term security, deserve neither freedom nor security.

➢ The purpose of money was to purchase one's freedom to pursue that which is useful and interesting.

➢ What is without us has no connection with happiness, only so far as the preservation of our lives and health depends upon it. . . . Happiness springs immediately from the mind.

➢ To the generous mind the heaviest debt is that of gratitude, when it is not in our power to repay it.

➢ Give me 26 lead soldiers and I will conquer the world.

➢ Rebellion to tyrants is obedience to God.

➢ Scarcely have I ever heard or read the introductory phrase, "I may say without vanity," but some striking and characteristic instance of vanity has immediately followed.

➢ If anyone should doubt whether the electrical matter passes through the substance of bodies, or only over along their surfaces, a shock from an electrified large glass jar, taken through his own body, will probably convince him.

➢ Outside Independence Hall when the Constitutional Convention of 1787 ended

➢ Conceiving God to be the fountain of wisdom, I thought it right and necessary to solicit his assistance for obtaining it.

➢ Electrical matter differs from common matter in this, that the parts of the latter mutually attract, those of the former mutually repel each other.

➢ The electrical matter consists of particles extremely subtile, since it can permeate common matter, even the densest metals, with such ease and freedom as not to receive any perceptible resistance.

➢ The only time not wasted is wasted time.

➢ Buy what thou hast no need of and ere long thou shalt sell thy necessities.

➢ The most trifling actions that affect a man's credit are to be regarded. The sound of your hammer at five in the morning, or at nine at night, heard by a creditor, makes him easy six months longer; but if he sees you at the billiard-table, or hears your voice at a tavern, when you should be at work, he sends for his money the next day.

➢ Kill no more pigeons than you can eat.

➢ Be in general virtuous, and you will be happy. At least, you will by such conduct, stand the best chance for such consequences.

➢ If we restrict liberty to attain security we will lose them both.

➢ My dear friend, do not imagine that I am vain enough to ascribe our success [Revolution] to any superiority . . . If it had not been for the justice of our cause, and the consequent interposition of Providence, in which we had faith, we must have been ruined. If I had ever before been an atheist, I should now have been

convinced of the being and government of a
Deity!

➢ If the new Universal History were also read, it
would give a connected idea of human affairs,
so far as it goes, which should be followed by
the best modern histories, particularly of our
mother country; then of these colonies; which
should be accompanied with observations on
their rise, increase, use to Great Britain,
encouragements and discouragements, the
means to make them flourish, and secure their
liberties.

➢ Savages we call them, because their manners
differ from ours, which we think the perfection
of civility; they think the same of theirs.

➢ The madness of mobs or the insolence of
soldiers, or both, when too near to each other,
occasion some mischief.

➢ The nearest I can make it out, "Love your
Enemies" means, "Hate your Friends"

➢ Nor is it of much Importance to us to know the
Manner in which Nature executes her laws; 'tis
enough to know the Laws themselves.

- Serving God is doing good to man, but praying is thought an easier service and therefore more generally chosen.

- I was put to the grammar-school at eight years of age, my father intending to devote me, as the tithe of his sons, to the service of the Church.

- Hast thou virtue? acquire also the graces and beauties of virtue.

- A [desire] to abolish slavery prevails in North America, many of the Pennsylvanians have set their slaves at liberty, and [Virginia legislators] have petitioned the King for permission to make a law for preventing the importation of more [slaves] into that colony. This request, however, will probably not be granted, as their former laws of that kind have always been repealed.

- An Episcopalian divine once told the Pope that the only difference between their denominations was that "the Church of Rome is infallible and the Church of England is never in the wrong."

- He who multiplies riches multiplies cares.

> A traveller should have a hog's nose, a deer's legs, and an ass's back.

> You must not, when you have gained a victory, use any triumphing or insulting expressions, nor show too much of the pleasure you feel; but endeavour to console your adversary, and make him less dissatisfied with himself by every kind and civil expression that may be used with truth; such as, you understand the game better than I, but you are a little inattentive, or, you play too fast; or, you had the best of the game, but something happened to divert your thoughts, and that turned it in my favour.

> A man is not completely born until he is dead. Why then should we grieve that a new child is born among the immortals, a new member added to their happy society?

> Give me yesterday's bread, this day's flesh, and last year's cider

> An autobiography usually reveals nothing bad about its writer except his memory.

➢ The things of this world take up too much of my time, of which indeed I have too little left, to undertake anything like a reformation in religion.

➢ What vast additions to the conveniences and comforts of living might mankind have acquired, if the money spent in wars had been employed in works of public utility; what an extension of agriculture even to the tops of our mountains; what rivers rendered navigable, or joined by canals; what bridges, aqueducts, new roads, and other public works, edifices, and improvements might not have been obtained by spending those millions in doing good, which in the last war have been spent in doing mischief.

➢ I scarce ever heard or saw the introductory words, "Without vanity I may say," etc., but some vain thing immediately followed.

➢ All cats look gray in the dark.

➢ He that doth what he should not, shall feel what he would not.

➢ To expect people to be good, to be just, to be temperate, etc., without showing them how

they should become so, seems like the
ineffectual charity mentioned by the apostle,
which consisted in saying to the hungry, the
cold and the naked, be ye fed, be ye warmed,
be ye clothed, without showing them how they
should get food, fire or clothing.

➤ ...till we are uneasy in Rest, we can have no
Desire to move, and without Desire of moving
there can be no voluntary Motion.

➤ But they have two other Rights; those of sitting
when they please, and as long as they please, in
which methinks they have the advantage of
your Parliament; for they cannot be dissolved
by the Breath of a Minister, or sent packing as
you were the other day, when it was your
earnest desire to have remained longer
together.

➤ The punishment of murder by death is contrary
to reason, and to the order and happiness of
society, and contrary to divine revelation.

➤ Saying and Doing, have quarrel'd and parted.

➤ As sore places meet most rubs, proud folks
meet most affronts.

> She that paints her Face, thinks of her Tail.

> I believe ... that the soul of man is immortal and will be treated with justice in another life, respecting its conduct in this.

> Indeed, when religious people quarrel about religion, or hungry people quarrel about victuals, it looks as if they had not much of either among them.

> Time is money, be a better you.

> A policy of life insurance is the cheapest and safest mode of making a certain provision for one's family.

> I've striven my whole life for humility, but if I'd ever achieved it, I'd probably be pretty damn proud of that.

> When religion is good, it will take care of itself. When it is not able to take care of itself, and God does not see fit to take care of it, so that it has to appeal to the civil power for support, it is evidence to my mind that its cause is a bad one.

- Gentlemen, I have lived a long time and am convinced that God governs in the affairs of men. If a sparrow cannot fall to the ground without His notice, is it probable that an empire can rise without His aid? I move that prayer imploring the assistance of Heaven be held every morning before we proceed to business.

- Slavery is ...an atrocious debasement of human nature.

- When in doubt, don't.

- The first mistake in public business is the going into it.

- A dying man can do nothing easy.

- Love and toothache have many cures, but none infallible, except possession and dispossession.

- Virtues, of ... Justice: Wrong none by doing injuries or omitting the benefits that are your duty.

- I say it is impossible that so sensible a people [citizens of Paris], under such circumstances, should have lived so long by the smoky, unwholesome, and enormously expensive light of candles, if they had really known that they might have had as much pure light of the sun for nothing.

➢ Let all Men know thee, but no man know thee thoroughly: Men freely ford that see the shallows.

➢ A man is not completely born until he is dead.

➢ Twas Noah who first planted the vine And mended his morals by drinking its wine.

➢ What is a butterfly? At best He's but a caterpiller drest. The gaudy Fop's his picture just.

➢ Those who prefer security to liberty deserve neither.

➢ The game of Chess is not merely an idle amusement; several very valuable qualities of the mind are to be acquired and strengthened by it, so as to become habits ready on all occasions, for life is a kind of chess.

➢ Most people dislike vanity in others, whatever share they have of it themselves; but I give it fair quarter, wherever I meet with it, being persuaded that it is often productive of good to the possessor, and to others who are within his sphere of action: and therefore, in many cases, it would not be altogether absurd if a man were to thank God for his vanity among the other comforts of life.

➢ All wars are follies, very expensive and very mischievous ones. In my opinion, there never was a good war or a bad peace. When will mankind be convinced and agree to settle their difficulties by arbitration?

➢ It is very imprudent to deprive America of any of her privileges. If her commerce and friendship are of any importance to you, they are to be had on no other terms than leaving her in the full enjoyment of her rights.

➢ A lady asked Dr. Franklin Well Doctor what have we got a republic or a monarchy - "A republic," replied the Doctor, "if you can keep it."

➢ That wise Men have in all Ages thought Government necessary for the Good of

Mankind; and, that wise Governments have always thought Religion necessary for the well ordering and well-being of Society, and accordingly have been ever careful to encourage and protect the Ministers of it, paying them the highest publick Honours, that their Doctrines might thereby meet with the greater Respect among the common People.

➢ God will certainly reward virtue and punish vice, either here or hereafter.

➢ Lawyers, Preachers, and Tomtits Eggs, there are more of them hatch'd than come to perfection.

➢ And as to the Cares, they are chiefly what attend the bringing up of Children; and I would ask any Man who has experienced it, if they are not the most delightful Cares in the World; and if from that Particular alone, he does not find the Bliss of a double State much greater, instead of being less than he expected.

➢ That it is better 100 guilty Persons should escape than that one innocent Person should suffer, is a Maxim that has been long and generally approved.

➢ To the haranguers of the populace among the ancients, succeed among the moderns your writers of political pamphlets and news-papers, and your coffee-house talkers.

➢ Thou can'st not joke an enemy into a friend, but thou may'st a friend into an enemy.

➢ I think with you, that nothing is of more importance for the public weal, than to form and train up youth in wisdom and virtue. Wise and good men are in my opinion, the strength of the state; more so than riches or arms.

➢ I am on this account not displeased that the Figure is not known as a Bald Eagle, but looks more like a Turkey. For the Truth the Turkey is in Comparison a much more respectable Bird, and withal a true original Native of America... He is besides, though a little vain & silly, a Bird of Courage, and would not hesitate to attack a Grenadier of the British Guards who should presume to invade his Farm Yard with a red Coat on.

➢ Duty is not beneficial because it is commanded, but is commanded because it is beneficial.

➢ Better is little with the fear of the Lord, than great treasure, and trouble therewith.

➢ Perhaps I was too saucy and provoking.

➢ Not to oversee workmen is to leave them your purse open.

➢ Those who are fear'd, are hated.

➢ Squeamish stomachs cannot eat without pickles.

➢ At the working man's house, hunger looks in but dares not enter.

➢ I grew convinced that truth, sincerity and integrity in dealings between man and man were of the utmost importance to the felicity of life, and I formed written resolutions . . . to practice them ever while I lived.

➢ We have no poor houses in the Colonies, and if we had, we would have no one to put in them, as in the Colonies there is not a single unemployed man, no poor and no vagabonds.

➢ I have met the enemy, and it is the eyes of other people.

➢ Those renowned generals [Alexander and Caesar] received more faithful service, and performed greater actions by means of the love their soldiers bore them, than they could possibly have done, if instead of being beloved and respected they had been hated and feared by those they commanded.

➢ He who will not be counseled cannot be helped.

➢ No nation has ever been ruined by trade.

➢ We can defer, yet time is most certainly not.

➢ 'Tis true there is much to be done, . . . but stick to it steadily, and you will see great effects, for constant dropping wears away stones . . . and little strokes fell great oaks, as Poor Richard says. . . .

➢ A virtuous and industrious people may be cheaply governed.

➢ Industry and frugality, as the means of procuring wealth . . . thereby [secures] virtue, it being more difficult for a man in want to act always honestly. . . .

➢ A fat kitchin, a lean Will.

➢ Gaining money by my industry and frugality, I lived very agreeably. . . .

➢ Let thy maid servant be faithful, strong, and homely.

➢ In every animal that walks upright, the deficiency of the Fluids that fill the Muscles appears first in the highest Part: The Face first grows lank and wrinkled; then the neck; then the breast and arms; the lower parts continuing to the last as plump as ever; so that covering all above with a basket, and regarding only what is below the girdle, it is impossible of two women to know an old from a young one.

➢ Great talkers, little doers.

➢ In humility imitate Jesus and Socrates.

➢ Masonic ideas are the precious jewels of Speculative Masons; the should be kept bright and sparkling for all the brethren to see and to admire. As such, they should be the special care of Masonic leaders particularly those who teach and interpret the philosophy of Freemasonry.

➢ Annual giving is the custom of making a gift-a-year to an institution in which one has faith.

➢ Pride is as loud a beggar as want, and a great deal more saucy

➢ Love of country is the Mason's deed; world citizenship is his thought.

➢ A greater Quantity of some things may be eaten than of others, some being of lighter Digestion than others.

➢ That Quantity that is sufficient, the Stomach can perfectly concoct and digest, and it sufficeth the due Nourishment of the Body.

➢ Fond pride of dress is sure a very curse

➢ Here's to our beloved George Washington, the Joshua of America, who commanded the sun and the moon to stand still - and they obeyed.

➢ The exact Quantity and Quality being found out,
is to be kept to constantly.

➢ 'tis his honesty that brought upon him the
character of a heretic.

➢ A wolf eats sheep but now and then, ten
Thousands are devour'd by Men.

➢ Prayers and Provender hinder no Journey.

➢ The States acceded to the Union.

➢ Every accent, every emphasis, every modulation
of voice, was so perfectly well turned and well
placed, that, without being interested in the
subject, one could not help being pleased with
the discourse; a pleasure of much the same kind
with that received from an excellent piece of
music. This is an advantage itinerant preachers
have over those who are stationary, as the
latter can not well improve their delivery of a
sermon by so many rehearsals.

➢ Great Modesty often hides great Merit.

➢ Don't overload Gratitude; if you do, she'll kick.

➢ Strange secrets are let out by Death Who blabs so oft the follies of this world.

➢ Pride gets into the Coach, and Shame mounts behind.

➢ Friends are the true Sceptres of Princes.

➢ Neglect kills injuries, revenge increases them.

➢ Don't halloo until you're out of the wood.

➢ Time Like a petal in the wind Flows softly by As old lives are taken New ones begin A continual chain Which lasts throughout eternity Every life but a minute in time But each of equal importance

➢ Nor eye in a letter, nor hand in a purse, nor ear in the secret of another.

➢ Many would live by their Wits, but break for want of Stock.

➢ Why should Pennsylvania, founded by the English, become a Colony of Aliens, who will shortly be so numerous as to Germanize us instead of our Anglifying them, and will never adopt our Language or Customs, any more than they can acquire our Complexion.

➢ The wise and the brave dares own that he was wrong.

➢ Grace thou thy house and let not that grace thee.

➢ Mankind naturally and generally love to be flatter'd.

➢ Seek virtue and of that posest, to Providence resign the rest.

➢ Anger warms the invention, but overheats the oven.

➢ Tolerate no Uncleanliness in Body, Clothes, or Habitation.

➢ That the vegetable creation should restore the air which is spoiled by the animal part of it, looks like a rational system, and seems to be of a piece with the rest.

➢ If all but myself were blind, I should want neither a fine house nor fine furniture.

- The good particular men may do separately, in relieving the sick, is small, compared with what they may do collectively.

- Private property...is the creature of society and is subject to the calls of that society even to the last farthing.

- A lonely man on a rainy night who cannot read.

- What's a Sun-Dial in the shade?

- Increase in me that wisdom Which discovers my truest interest, Strengthen my resolution To perform that which wisdom dictates.

- I know as well as thee that I am no poet born It is a trade, I never learnt nor indeed could learn If I make verses-'tis in spite Of nature and my stars I write.

- There is no gains without pain.

- an enormous proportion of property vested in a few individuals is dangerous to the rights, and destructive of the common happiness of mankind, and, therefore, every free state hath a right by its laws to discourage the possession of such property.

➢ Nothing in the world is certain except for death and taxes.

➢ It is easier to build two chimneys than to keep one in fuel.

➢ He that drinks fast, pays slow. Beer is proof that God loves us and wants us to be happy. There can't be good living where there is not good drinking.

➢ What more valuable than Gold? Diamonds. Than Diamonds? Virtue.

➢ Lazy bones! Dost thou think God would have given thee arms and legs, if he had not design'd thou should'st use them?

➢ Life is a kind of chess.

➢ The importation of foreigners into a country that has as many inhabitants as the present employments and provisions for subsistence will bear, will be in the end no increase of people, unless the new comers have more industry and frugality than the natives, and then they will provide more subsistence, and increase in the country; but they will gradually eat the natives out. Nor is it necessary to bring in foreigners to fill up any occasional vacancy in a country for such vacancy will soon be filled by natural generation.

➢ Knowledge of the investment is most profitable

➢ It might be judged an affront to your understanding should I go about to prove this first principle; the existence of a Diety and that He is the Creator of the universe, for that would suppose you ignorant of what all mankind in all ages have agreed in.

➢ Virtues, of ... Moderation: Avoid extremes. Forbear resenting injuries so much as you think they deserve.

➢ On second thought, it's a good thing love is blind otherwise it would see too much.

➢ Necessity is our quickest excuse.

➢ Willows are weak, but they bind the Faggot.

- If you want to be rich, think of the savings and get them.

- It is the duty of mankind on all suitable occasions to acknowledge their dependence on the Divine Being.

- By the word simplicity, is not always meant folly or ignorance; but often, pure and upright Nature, free from artifice, craft or deceitful ornament.

- The pleasures of this world are rather from God's goodness than our own merit.

- Often I sit up in my room reading the greatest part of the night, when the book was borrowed in the evening and to be returned early in the morning, lest it should be missed or wanted.

- When about 16 Years of Age, I happened to meet with a Book written by one Tryon, recommending a Vegetable Diet. I determined to go into it.... My refusing to eat Flesh occasioned an inconveniency, and I was frequently chid for my singularity.

- ➢ You have two choices, write about something of significance or do something someone wants to write about.

- ➢ The greatest inventions are those inquiries which tend to increase the power of man over matter.

- ➢ All who think cannot but see there is a sanction like that of religion which binds us in partnership in the serious work of the world.

- ➢ People want to catch a buzz. That is why drugs are illegal, yet people still try to get their hands on them no matter what the consequence. Drugs make us happy, they may not be healthy.

- ➢ Eat to please thyself, but dress to please others.

- ➢ Never take a wife till thou hast a house (and a fire) to put her in.

- ➢ I guess I don't so much mind being old, as I mind being fat and old.

- ➢ And whether you're an honest man, or whether you're a thief, depends on whose solicitor has given me my brief.

- ➢ Savages we call them because their manners differ from ours.

- ➢ When befriended, remember it; when you befriend, forget it.

- ➢ In the affairs of this world, men are saved not by faith, but by the want of it.

- ➢ When men and woman die, as poets sung, his heart's the last part moves, her last, the tongue.

- ➢ Who had deceived thee so often as thyself?

- ➢ Since thou are not sure of a minute, throw not away an hour.

- ➢ Gain may be temporary and uncertain; but ever while you live, expense is constant and certain: and it is easier to build two chimneys than to keep one in fuel.

- ➢ Those who govern, having much business on their hands, do not generally like to take the trouble of considering and carrying into execution new projects. The best public measures are therefore seldom adopted from previous wisdom, but forced by the occasion.

➢ Employ thy time well, if thou meanest to gain leisure.

➢ It's better to swim in the sea below Than to swing in the air and feed the crow, Says jolly Ned Teach of Bristol.

➢ Industry need not wish.

➢ Old boys have their playthings as well as young ones; the difference is only in the price.

➢ Liberality is not giving much, but giving wisely.

➢ From a child I was fond of reading, and all the little money that came into my hands was ever laid out in books.

➢ If Jack's in love, he's no judge of Jill's beauty.

➢ You have on hand those things that you need if you have but the wit and wisdom to use them.

➢ Perhaps I'm too saucy or provoking?

➤ powerful goodness! Bountiful Father! Merciful Guide! Increase in me that wisdom which discovers my truest interest. Strengthen my resolution to perform what that wisdom dictates. Accept my kind offices to thy other children as the only return in my power for thy continual favours to me.

➤ This gave me occasion to observe, that when Men are employ'd they are best contented. For on the Days they work'd they were good-natur'd and chearful; and with the consciousness of having done a good Days work they spent the Evenings jollily; but on the idle Days they were mutinous and quarrelsome, finding fault with their Pork, the Bread, and in continual ill-humour. (Autobiography, 1771)

➤ There was great difference in persons; and discretion did not always accompany years, nor was youth always without it.

➤ Half-wits talk much, but say little.

➤ Laziness travels so slowly that poverty soon overtakes it.

➤ A friend in need is a friend indeed!

➤ Let thy discontents be thy secrets

➤ The happy State of Matrimony is, undoubtedly, the surest and most lasting Foundation of Comfort and Love . . . the Cause of all good Order in the World, and what alone preserves it from the utmost Confusion.

➤ He that blows the coals in quarrels that he has nothing to do with, has no right to complain if the sparks fly in his face. - Ben Franklin

➤ Fish & Visitors stink in 3 days.

➤ Tis a well spent penny that saves a groat.

➤ Were the offer made true, I would engage to run again, from beginning to end, the same career of life. All I would ask should be the privilege of an author, to correct, in a second edition, certain errors of the first.

➤ Time eateth all things, could old poets say, The times are chang'd, our times drink all away.

➤ He that by the Plough would thrive, Himself must either hold or drive.

- Take courage, Mortal... Death cannot banish you from the Universe.

- Pity and forbearance should characterize all acts of justice.

- Wealth and Content are not always Bed-fellows.

- The English love an insult. It's their only test of a man's sincerity.

- Ambition has its disappointments to sour us, but never the good fortune to satisfy us.

- Never praise your cider or your horse

- Mary's mouth cost her nothing for she never opens it but at others' expense.

- A little Religion, and a little Honesty, goes a great way in Courts.

- The good or ill hap of a good or ill life, is the good or ill choice of a good or ill wife.

➢ Epitaph on a scolding wife by her husband: Here my poor Bridget's corpse doth lie, she is at rest - and so am I!

➢ In a discreet man's mouth, a public thing is private.

➢ He that won't be counseled can't be helped. He that would have a short Lent, let him borrow Money to be repaid at Easter.

➢ When I see nothing annihilated, and not even a drop of water wasted, I cannot suspect the annihilation of souls Thus finding myself to exist in the world, I believe I shall, in some shape or other, always exist; with all the inconveniences human life is liable to, I shall not object to a new edition of mine; hoping, however, that the errata of the last may be corrected.

➢ Never contradict anybody.

➢ I am what I am and that's all that I am and if I'm supposed to be somebody else, why do I look like me?

➢ Mankind are dastardly when they meet with opposition.

➢ Covetousness is ever attended with solicitude and anxiety.

➢ Onions can make even Heirs and Widows weep.

➢ If we can sleep without dreaming, it is well that painful dreams are avoided. If, while we sleep, we can have any pleasing dreams, it is as the French say, tant gagne, so much added to the pleasure of life.

➢ Speak and speed: the close mouth catches no flies.

➢ The riches of a country are to be valued by the quantity of labor its inhabitants are able to purchase, and not by the quantity of silver and gold they possess; which will purchase more or less labor, and therefore is more or less valuable, as is said before, according to its scarcity or plenty.

➢ Reckless haste makes poor speed.

➢ Notwithstanding my experiments with electricity the thunderbolt continues to fall under our noses and beards; and as for the tyrant, there are a million of us still engaged at snatching away his sceptre.

➢ Christianity commands us to pass by injuries; policy, to let them pass by us.

➢ Christians are directed to have faith in Christ, as the effectual means of obtaining the change they desire.

➢ There is much money given to be laughed at, though the purchasers don't know it; witness A.'s fine horse, and B.'s fine house.

➢ At a great pennyworth pause a while.

➢ No better relation than a prudent and faithful friend.

➢ Here you would know, and enjoy, what prosperity will way of Washington. For a thousand leagues have nearly the same effect with a thousand years.

➢ Take care of the halfpence and pence, and the shillings and pounds will take care of themselves.

➢ Most people dislike vanity in others, whatever share they have of it themselves.

➢ We may perhaps learn to deprive large masses of their gravity and give them absolute levity, for the sake of easy transport.

➢ But in this world nothing is sure but death and taxes. [Fr., Mais dons ce monde, il n'y a rien d'assure que le mort et les impots.]

➢ That as we enjoy great advantages from the inventions of others, we should be glad of an opportunity to serve others by any invention of ours, and this we should do freely and generously.

➢ By my rambling digressions I perceive myself to be growing old.

➢ The electrical matter consists of particles extremely subtile, since it can permeate common matter, even the densest metals, with such ease and freedom as not to receive any perceptible resistance. If anyone should doubt whether the electrical matter passes through the substance of bodies, or only over along their surfaces, a shock from an electrified large glass jar, taken through his own body, will probably convince him. Electrical matter differs from common matter in this, that the parts of the latter mutually attract, those of the former mutually repel each other.

➢ An infallible Remedy for the Tooth-ach, viz Wash the Root of an aching Tooth, in Elder Vinegar, and let it dry half an hour in the Sun; after which it will never ach more; Probatum est.

➢ Anyone willing to give up liberty in exchange for security deserves neither.

➢ What signifies Philosophy that does not apply to some Use? May we not learn from hence, that black Clothes are not so fit to wear in a hot Sunny Climate or Season, as white ones; because in such Cloaths the Body is more heated by the Sun when we walk abroad, and are at the same time heated by the Exercise, which double Heat is apt to bring on putrid dangerous Fevers? The Soldiers and Seamen, who must march and labour in the Sun, should in the East or West Indies have an Uniform of white?

➢ We are not certain, we are never certain. If we were we could reach some conclusions, and we could, at last, make others take us seriously. In this world nothing can be said to be certain, except death and taxes.

➢ He that resolves to mend hereafter, resolves not to mend now.

➢ Philosophy as well as foppery often changes fashion.

➢ Those who sacrifice essential liberty for temporary safety are not deserving of either liberty or safety.

➢ Dally not with other folk's spouses or money.

➢ He that scatters thorns, let him not go barefoot.

➢ Moses lifting up his wand, and dividing the Red Sea, and Pharaoh in his chariot overwhelmed with the waters. This motto: "Rebellion to tyrants is obedience to God."

➢ He is ill clothed that is bare of virtue.

➢ Quarrels never could last long, if on one side only lay the wrong.

➢ People who are wrapped up in themselves make small packages.

➢ Life is rather a state of embryo, a preparation for life; a man is not completely born till he has passed through death.

➢ Before Noah, men having only water to drink, could not find the truth. Accordingly...they became abominably wicked, and they were justly exterminated by the water they loved to drink. This good man, Noah, having seen that all his contemporaries had perished by this unpleasant drink, took a dislike to it; and God, to relieve his dryness, created the vine and revealed to him the art of making le vin. By the aid of this liquid he unveiled more and more truth.

➢ To be thrown upon one's own resources is to be cast into the very lap of fortune; for our faculties then undergo a development and display an energy of which they were previosly unsusceptible.

➢ Our new Constitution is now established, and has an appearance that promises permanency; but in the world nothing can be said to be certain except death and taxes.

➢ Wouldst thou enjoy a long Life, a healthy Body, and a vigorous Mind, and be acquainted also with the wonderful Works of God? labour in the first place to bring thy Appetite into Subjection to Reason.

➢ Nothing is more important for the public wealth than to form and train youth in wisdom and virtue. Only a virtuous people are capable of freedom.

➢ The Body of B. Franklin, Printer Like the Cover of an old Book Its Contents turn out And Stript of its Lettering & Guilding Lies here. Food for Worms For, it will as he believed appear once more In a new and more elegant Edition corrected and improved By the Author.

➢ It seems to me, that if statesmen had a little more arithmetic, or were accustomed to calculation, wars would be much less frequent.

➢ Who has deceived thee as oft as thyself.

➢ A cheerful face is nearly as good for an invalid as healthy weather.

➢ I have been apt to think that there has never been, nor ever will be, any such thing as a good war, or a bad peace.

➢ To inquisitive minds like yours and mine the reflection that the quantity of human knowledge bears no proportion to the quantity of human ignorance must be in one view rather pleasing, viz., that though we are to live forever we may be continually amused and delighted with learning something new.

➢ The sun of liberty is set; you must light up the candle of industry and economy.

➢ I have heard that nothing gives an Author so great Pleasure, as to find his works respectfully quoted by other learned authors.

➢ In going on with these Experiments, how many pretty systems do we build, which we soon find ourselves oblig'd to destroy! If there is no other Use discover'd of Electricity, this, however, is something considerable, that it may help to make a vain Man humble.

➢ You and I were long friends: you are now my enemy, and I am yours.

➢ He that sells upon Credit expects to lose 5 per Cent. By bad Debts; therefore he charges, on all he sells upon Credit, an Advance that shall make up that Deficiency.

➢ What one relishes, nourishes.

➢ A fine genius in his own country is like gold in the mine.

➢ 'Tis more noble to forgive, and more manly to despise, than to revenge an Injury.

➢ Do not, however, mistake me. It is not to my good friend's heresy that I impute his honesty. On the contrary, 'tis his honesty that brought upon him the character of a heretic.

➢ It is wonderful how preposterously the affairs of the world are managed. We assemble parliaments and councils to have the benefit of collected wisdom, but we necessarily have, at the same time, the inconvenience of their collected passions, prejudices and private interests: for regulating commerce an assembly of great men is the greatest fool on earth

- Hereafter, if you should observe an occasion to give your officers and friends a little more praise than is their due, and confess more fault than you can justly be charged with, you will only become the sooner for it, a great captain.

- Cheese and salt meat, should be sparingly eat.

- I looked around for God's judgments, but saw no signs of them.

- Use now and then a little Exercise a quarter of an Hour before Meals, as to swing a Weight, or swing your Arms about with a small Weight in each Hand; to leap, or the like, for that stirs the Muscles of the Breast.

- Grief for a dead Wife, and a troublesome Guest, Continues to the threshold, and there is at rest; But I mean such wives as are none of the best

- Poverty, Poetry, and new Titles of Honor, make Men ridiculous

➢ Here Skugg lies snug As a bug in a rug.

➢ Nothing's so apt to undermine your confidence in a product as knowing that the commercial selling it has been approved by the company that makes it.

➢ Make no expense but to do good to others or yourself.

➢ If you would know the value of money; go, and try to borrow some! For, he that goes a borrowing, goes a sorrowing! and indeed, so does he that lends to such people, when he goes to get it in again!

➢ A man separated from his reflective belt is no man at all.

➢ It was said of him that he did not say much, but that when he did everyone stopped to listen.

➢ The Honey is sweet, but the Bee has a Sting.

➢ There's many witty men whose brains can't fill their bellies.

> ➢ I think that a young state, like a young virgin, should modestly stay at home, and wait the application of suitors for an alliance with her; and not run about offering her amity to all the world; and hazarding their refusal. Our virgin is a jolly one; and tho at present not very rich, will in time be a great fortune, and where she has a favorable predisposition, it seems to me well worth cultivating.

> ➢ Evils come not, then our fears are vain; And if they do fear but augments the pain.

> ➢ A father's a treasure; a brother's a comfort; a friend is both.

> ➢ If a man would reap praise, you must sow the seeds, gentle words and useful deeds.

> ➢ Have you something to do to-morrow; do it to-day.

> ➢ Some books we read, tho' few there are that hit the happy point where wisdom joins with wit.

> ➢ If your riches are yours, why don't you take them with you to the other world?

- ➤ Remember, that money is of the prolific, generating nature.

- ➤ Whenever we attempt to mend the scheme of Providence and to interfere in the Government of the world, we had need be very circumspect lest we do more harm than good.

- ➤ Drink does not drown care, but waters it, and makes it grow faster.

- ➤ An iron rod being placed on the outside of a building from the highest part continued down into the moist earth, in any direction strait or crooked, following the form of the roof or other parts of the building, will receive the lightning at its upper end, attracting it so as to prevent it's striking any other part; and, affording it a good conveyance into the earth, will prevent its damaging any part of the building.

- ➤ Let every one ascertain his special business and calling, and then stick to it if he wants to be successful.

- ➤ We are a kind of posterity in respect to them.

➢ If a sound body and a sound mind, which is as much as to say health and virtue, are to be preferred before all other considerations, ought not men, in choosing a business either for themselves or children, to refuse such as are unwholesome for the body, and such as make a man too dependent, too much obliged to please others, and too much subjected to their humors in order to be recommended and get a livelihood?

➢ That which resembles most living one's life over again, seems to be to recall all the circumstances of it; and, to render this remembrance more durable, to record them in writing.

➢ The Golden Age was never the present age.

➢ And we daily in our experiments electrise bodies plus or minus, as we think proper. [These terms we may use till your Philosophers give us better.] To electrise plus or minus, no more needs to be known than this, that the parts of the Tube or Sphere, that are rubb'd, do, in the Instant of Friction, attract the Electrical Fire, and therefore take it from the Thin rubbing; the same parts immediately, as the Friction upon them ceases, are disposed to give the fire they have received, to any Body that has less.

> The only things of certainty are Death and Taxes.

> Many estates are spent in the getting, since women for tea forsake spinning and knitting, and men for punch forsake hewing and splitting.

> Hope and faith may be more firmly built upon charity, than charity upon faith and hope.

> Getting into debt, is getting into a tanglesome net.

> He that's content hath enough.

> Furnished as all Europe now is with Academies of Science, with nice instruments and the spirit of experiment, the progress of human knowledge will be rapid and discoveries made of which we have at present no conception. I begin to be almost sorry I was born so soon, since I cannot have the happiness of knowing what will be known a hundred years hence.

➢ Idleness is the Dead Sea that swallows all virtues. Be active in business, that temptation may miss her aim; the bird that sits is easily shot.

➢ He that speaks ill of the mare will buy her.

➢ Certainlie these things agree, The Priest, the Lawyer, & Death all three: Death takes both the weak and the strong. The lawyer takes from both right and wrong, And the priest from living and dead has his Fee.

➢ Men differ daily about things which are subject to sense, is it likely then they should agree about things invisible.

➢ As to the kindness you mention, I wish I could have been of more service to you than I have been, but if I had, the only thanks that I should desire are that you would always be ready to serve any other person that may need your assistance, and so let good offices go around, for humankind are all of a family. As for my own part, when I am employed in serving others I do not look upon myself as conferring favors but paying debts.

➢ If Pride leads the Van, Beggary brings up the
Rear.

➢ Beer is God's way of telling us that he loves us
and wants us to be happy.

➢ By diligence and patience, the mouse bit in two
the cable.

➢ A wicked Hero will turn his back to an innocent
coward.

➢ God bless the King, and grant him long to Reign.

➢ The generous Mind least regards money, and
yet most feels the Want of it.

➢ Keep out of the Sight of Feasts and Banquets as
much as may be; for 'tis more difficult to refrain
good Cheer, when it's present, than from the
Desire of it when it is away; the like you may
observe in the Objects of all the other Senses.

➢ What you would seem to be, be really.

➢ The most exquisite folly is made of wisdom
spun too fine.

➢ If principle is good for anything, it is worth living up to.

➢ Man is a tool-making animal

➢ "We hold these truths to be sacred and undeniable" in a draft of the Declaration of Independence changes it instead into an assertion of rationality. The scientific mind of Franklin drew on the scientific determinism of Isaac Newton and the analytic empiricism of David Hume and Gottfried Leibniz. In what became known as "Hume's Fork" the latters' theory distinguished between synthetic truths that describe matters of fact, and analytic truths that are self-evident by virtue of reason and definition.

➢ None are deceived but they that confide.

➢ What science can there be more noble, more excellent, more useful for men, more admirably high and demonstrative, than this of mathematics?

➢ [It was] the poverty caused by the bad influence of the English bankers on the Parliament which has caused in the colonies hatred of the English and . . . the Revolutionary War.

➢ My refusing to eat flesh occasioned an inconveniency, and I was frequently chid for my singularity.

➢ Write with the learned, pronounce with the vulgar.

➢ If this lady is pleased to spend her days with Franklin, he would be just as pleased to spend his nights with her.

➢ A child thinks 20 shillings and 20 years can never be spent.

➢ Those who are content have enough; those that complain, have too much.

➢ Remember this Saying, 'That the good Paymaster is Lord of another Man's Purse.' He that is known to pay punctually and exactly to the Time he promises, may at any Time, and on any Occasion, raise all the Money his Friends can spare.

- ➢ What maintains one vice would bring up two children.

- ➢ Our friend and we were invited aboard on a party of pleasure, which is to last forever. His chair was ready first, and he has gone before us. We could not all conveniently start together; and why should you and I be grieved at this, since we are soon to follow, and know where to find him.

- ➢ Ben Franklin was a little stout later in life and it was said that in Paris a young woman, tapping him on his protruding abdomen, said,"Dr. Franklin, if this were on a woman, we'd know what to think." And Franklin replied,"Half an hour ago, Mademoiselle, it was on a woman, and now what do you think?"

- ➢ He that riseth late, must trot all day, and shall scarce overtake his business at night.

- ➢ In truth I found myself incorrigible with respect to Order; and now I am grown old, and my Memory bad, I feel very sensibly the want of it.